Captain Billy's Troopers

Captain Billy with his family at Gulf Shores in August 1946.

Captain Billy's Troopers

A Writer's Life

WILLIAM COBB

The University of Alabama Press
Tuscaloosa

The University of Alabama Press
Tuscaloosa, Alabama 35487–0380
uapress.ua.edu

Typeface: Janson

Manufactured in the United States of America
Cover photograph: © Sushi King - Fotolia.com
Design: Michele Myatt Quinn

∞
The paper on which this book is printed meets the minimum requirements of American National Standard for Information Sciences—Permanence of Paper for Printed Library Materials, ANSI Z39.48–1984.

Library of Congress Cataloging-in-Publication Data

Cobb, William, 1937–
Captain Billy's troopers : a writer's life / William Cobb.
pages cm
Includes index.
ISBN 978-0-8173-1876-5 (hardback) — ISBN 978-0-8173-8875-1 (e book) 1. Cobb, William, 1937– 2. Authors, American—20th century—Biography. 3. Alcoholism—Biography. 4. Storytelling—Alabama. 5. Hydrocephalus. I. Title.
PS3553.O198Z46 2015
813'.54—dc23
[B]

2015000665

For Sidney Vance

On a spring evening in the mid-1950s, on a narrow two-lane thinly paved county road through fields green and bursting with new life, a 1952 Chevy coupe, red top, black chassis, rips by, going very fast. Inside is packed a group of boys and girls, singing loudly and laughing happily with vigorous abandon. They are drunk. Drunk with alcohol and with being young and alive. They are singing, "We're Captain Billy's Troopers, we're riders of the night." Their voices linger long after the car is gone, disappearing over the hill toward home.

One

It was almost midnight on July 21, 1984, as I sat in the admitting office at Brookwood Hospital in Birmingham. I was in a state of suspended consciousness, unable to fully comprehend that this was really happening to me. I was angry. The admitting officer had just informed me that I could not be admitted without a physician's referral. I was shaking. My mouth was sticky dry. I was in bad shape. My confused mind was conflicted: Okay, I can go home and get a drink, which I sorely needed. But I was here, I had taken this step. I had steeled myself up like preparing to jump off a cliff and I didn't want it to be for nothing.

My good friend Sid Vance was just outside the door listening. I insisted they admit me. I asked them if they couldn't see that I was in need of medical care. I was drunk enough to stand up to them. "Goddamit," I said, "I'm not leaving this chair until you admit me into this hospital." There was something oddly comforting about being there; it was orderly, quiet, and cool. I didn't want to go back to that empty house. I was defiant. People came and went, conferring in whispers. "We have contacted Dr. White," they finally said, "and he is admitting you." I had no idea who the hell Dr. White was and I didn't care.

I hugged Sidney and said good-bye to him in the lobby. I thanked him. I could tell he was frightened for me, almost as scared as I was. I didn't know what they would do to me or for me. I just knew that when I came off the booze, I'd be under the care of people who knew what was happening. I knew what coming down from the booze was like, the seizures, the trembling, the terrors. I wanted to be in a doctor's care when it happened, because I knew that I could die. Once, when my wife and I had been driving back from Vermont, I'd had a terrifying episode. I had thought I might die. I had been nursing a buzz all summer long, never more than arm's reach from a beer or a drink. We left Bread Loaf in the early morning and drove all the way to a little motel we liked in Brewster, New York, arriving in the late afternoon. I had nothing to drink all day. When we got there, I began to feel the seizure coming on. I asked Loretta to take care of the registering. When she went into the office, I began to shake uncontrollably. I could see, in the rearview mirror, that my eyes were contorted and my skin was pale and pasty. I fumbled around behind the seat and found a bottle of bourbon. I was going to pour me a drink in a plastic cup, but my hands were jumping around so badly I couldn't hold it. I was gasping. I couldn't get my breath. I knew I'd spill whiskey all over the car. So I just turned the bottle up and sucked it like a baby bottle. I could feel the liquor burning. I could feel my pulse begin to calm. After a few minutes the shaking subsided. By the time Loretta got back to the car, the seizure was over. I knew that liquor would kill me. But I had to have liquor to be alive.

This time, this latest binge, I'd been alone in the house for about two weeks. Loretta had taken Meredith and gone to her mother's and then on to our nephew's house in Georgia. I had rarely taught my classes during that time. I had a kindly graduate assistant who filled in for me. That she was enabling me is now beside the point; she was saving my job. Loretta was the one doing the "tough loving." "I'm not leaving you, I love you," she'd said, "but I can't live like this. Do something about your drinking. So I can come back." She was firm. I knew she meant it.

But I could not stop. The future was like a dark, icy tunnel into nothingness, and it was as though I were in a warm feather bed, and when I tried to get up and saw that bleak future, I fell back. Except that where I was was hardly a warm feather bed. It was a pit of horror. *Depression* is an inadequate word. I was so full of sorrow and revulsion and anger I could not function and I had to have alcohol to shut out all those emotions.

I knew that I couldn't face the rest of my life without booze. I had plenty. I slept whenever I wanted to. I had little appetite. After a week, I vomited whatever I tried to put into my stomach. I vomited blood and it terrified me. I would wake up at two or three in the morning and pad through the house to snort more whiskey.

I had no more food in the house so, as drunk as I was, I drove to the Piggly Wiggly. In my befuddled state I bought instant potatoes, reasoning that they would be simple to make and easy on my stomach. I puked them up. I had long ago left that time when drinking was pleasurable, fun; now it was a medicinal necessity to even feel normal. Every morning was a struggle to get to that point: to quiet the tremors and the demons until I could sit quietly and feel human. But I could no longer recognize that state of equilibrium even if I were to achieve it. I would slide over it quickly and sink again into the morass.

I missed Loretta and Meredith terribly. I tried to watch sports on TV but I couldn't follow them well. I drifted in an alcohol fog. Then I ran out of booze. By that time I could no longer drive. At least I had sense enough to know that. I called my friend Sidney Vance. He was alarmed at my state. I told him that I had to have a bottle of Scotch. He tried to talk me out of it. Finally he said all right, if that's what I wanted, he would get it for me. He brought me a bottle of Scotch and we talked.

I could see the concern and the compassion in his eyes. There was no judgment. If I wanted to kill myself, he would help me do it. But it broke his heart, because he loved me. I had hit my rock bottom. And with it came this recognition: A drunk grows old alone and dies alone, all alone, because all he wants is his booze and his booze seals him off from everything he values and loves. But there was a tiny glimmer of hope. Loretta and Meredith were still connected to me by the thinnest of threads. And Sidney was there. I asked him if he would drive me to the hospital. Of course he would.

I had my first beer when I was sixteen years old, in the back room of Red's Riverside Inn across the Warrior River from Demopolis, Alabama. Red's Riverside Inn was an African-American beer joint with a room in the back for whites. I loved beer from the start, from the first sip. I liked the feeling of being high, of easing away and up, and I liked the taste.

I was working for Henry Webb at the Marengo Theater as a general, all-around employee: I worked behind the candy counter, sold popcorn, worked the colored balcony on Saturday, drove around changing the little poster signs for movies in various venues around town, movies for the Marengo and the Grove Drive In, where I also worked from time to time.

I was allowed to drive my mother's car, and my father had a used Plymouth on the lot out at his car dealership that he let me borrow sometimes. I worked at night and on weekends, so I didn't date very much. A lot of the kids in my class "went steady," but I never did until later, when I entered a serious relationship in college. I had crushes, but they were usually on the most attractive girls in school, the ones the tall, good-looking athletes took out, so I suffered quite a bit from unrequited love. I was popular; girls seemed to like me, but "not in that way," always like a brother or good friend. By the time I was sixteen, most of the girls I knew were as tall as I was, some taller. I was short and stocky, and that's the way I was treated, as a short, stocky guy. I was a virgin, with no immediate prospects to changing that situation.

I couldn't really conceive of having sex with a girl. I could imagine it, of course (I was an avid masturbator), but it remained always at the level of fantasy. I did not believe that nice girls had sex. I don't think I was ever told overtly that sex was nasty and guilt-charged, but I acquired that knowledge somehow. Part of it, I suppose, was coming of age in the uptight fifties, that time of twin beds for married couples in movies, but most of the kids I knew seemed to have a healthier attitude toward all that than I did, or that was my perception. I actually believed other boys, older boys, when they regaled me with tales of their sexual conquests; the stories fired my fantasies. Maybe I wasn't so entirely alone in all that. A few years ago a friend, a guy I graduated from high school with, said to me at a cocktail party, "Billy, did you really screw ________?" He'd named one of those popular girls everybody, including me, had a crush on. He had an earnest, pleading look on his face, as though he wanted me to say yes. I told him that no, I hadn't screwed her. But I was flattered that he thought I had.

I knew I didn't fit in with the rougher, more adventurous boys, but I tried. I pretended to be like them. Everybody else seemed to know so much more about everything—especially sex—than I did. I paid attention—too much, probably—to what went on around me, what was said. I took it in, but it was fragmentary and perplexing. There were so many things that I didn't understand that I was hesitant to ask about. Things that I thought if I asked one of the older boys, I would get laughed at, exposed as a naif. I brooded. I was moody. It never occurred to me to ask an adult about anything. The minister at our cold, soulless Presbyterian church was elderly and stiff, distant, not someone who offered any kind of moral guidance that I could see, certainly not the kind of warm acceptance that I needed. My Boy Scout leader was a silly doofus. I had at least one coach that I admired, but I never would have tried to talk with him about anything personal.

Teachers were only to teach you stuff in school. I knew that I was on my own, that that's the way it was. I puzzled over hearing some of my friends who were Methodists going on about their minister, who was younger and apparently much more approachable, but I dismissed it because I thought he was an egotistical cornball. I didn't really want an older mentor; most of the older men I knew seemed obtuse, either distant and withdrawn or all bluster and hollow talk. I learned early on—for better or for worse—that the only person I could rely on was myself. For my whole life I would have a hard time looking to anyone else for guidance. If I trusted in the wrong—or the right—of a situation, it was because I trusted in only myself. That makes for a lonely journey.

Two

On June 4, 1977, I was in Williamstown, Massachusetts, visiting Kurt Heinzleman and Gill Bidlack, friends from the Bread Loaf days of several years earlier. I was on my way to Bennington College, just across the state line in Vermont, for a summer writing program with John Gardner and Nicholas Delbanco. I had left home in the early morning two days prior, in my green Triumph TR-7, had driven all the way to Scranton on the first day, then up into Massachusetts to Kurt and Gill's house on the previous day.

All the way up, on that grueling and gorgeous drive through the Shenandoah Valley, all alone in my little car, the image of Loretta and Meredith as I'd last glimpsed them lingered in my mind. Meredith was two years old then and Loretta held her in her arms as they waved good-bye to me in the driveway of our house in Montevallo, Alabama. I had left with moist eyes and heavy anxiety. I was nervous about this new adventure. Loretta was not happy that I was going. I was sure she was growing impatient with my ambition to succeed as a writer. I had published a handful of short stories—one of them, "The Stone Soldier," a national prize winner with *Story* magazine—and had completed two novels that I'd had no success in publishing, even with the help of two very good literary agents, Theron Raines and Al Zuckerman. I felt stuck, as though I'd run up against a solid wall, and I nursed nagging feelings of inadequacy, a lack of confidence in my own talent. I was suffering a growing suspicion that I was a fool, a naive loser, fooling only myself, while everybody else, especially Loretta and the rest of my family and friends, realized the truth and looked on me with amusement and pity.

Back during the early spring I had had John Gardner as a visiting writer at Montevallo, and we hit it off well. Gardner had recently had some very successful novels, *October Light*, *The Sunlight Dialogues*, and others. I liked him, though Loretta didn't. He drank too much and was brusque and, Loretta felt, rude. He offered out of the blue to read something of mine and I gave him the manuscript of *Coming of Age at the Y*, a comic novel. He liked the novel and wrote me some nice notes on it.

John wore jeans, sweatshirts, and heavy motorcycle boots. He didn't smell very good. He smoked a pipe and had long flowing bright blond hair that hung down his back in a tangled shag. He was from Batavia, New York, and he spoke with a clipped, upstate New England accent. Over the course of his several days in Montevallo, giving a reading and meeting with my writing workshop, drinking with me, we became fairly good friends, and he was encouraging to me. I grasped at his support. I had often felt very much alone and isolated in Montevallo, and here was one of the finest fiction writers in America (and the author of *The Art of Fiction* and *On Becoming a Novelist*, two of the best books on fiction writing ever written) praising my work and treating me like an equal, a peer. He told me about an eight-week writing workshop he was conducting the next summer at Bennington College in Vermont with the novelist Nicholas Delbanco and urged me to come to it, so that we could talk revision strategies on the novel and work on my fiction in general. He was enthusiastic about the workshop and quite persuasive. He said I would like Nick and we would all have a great time.

It was expensive. It would mean I'd be gone from home most of the summer. At the time I was dry (not *sober*, though I might have called myself sober then, erroneously); I had gone for two or three months—since right after John's visit—without a drink, which I would do from time to time, each time with the intention of quitting drinking for good. A drunk will do that. He will quit and assure you that this time it is for good. Yes, he is lying, but he does not know he's lying.

So when I promised Loretta that I was not going to drink, that I was going to stay clean and sober over the course of the summer, I really believed that. I believed it right up until on my second evening with Kurt and Gill I calmly accepted a Scotch on the rocks, and sitting with them in folding chairs in the backyard while Kurt grilled steaks, I drank along with them in the most natural, normal way, having some laughs and relaxing with good friends. Sitting on a crisp New England June evening, sipping sweet Scotch, while all those miles away down in Alabama, Loretta and Meredith went about their supper and the preparations for Meredith's bedtime.

To Kurt and Gill, it was like Bread Loaf, six years earlier. To *me*, it was like Bread Loaf, six years earlier. It even smelled like Bread Loaf, with the Vermont state line and its dense forests only a few miles to the north of where we were sitting. I knew I would experience the same kind of anxiety attacks at Bennington that I'd experienced at Bread Loaf, a paralyzing sensation of being totally off my turf, of being somewhere that I did not belong, where I did not fit, in a circumstance over which I had no control at all. I had suffered the same apprehensions years earlier when I was in graduate school at Vanderbilt; if I walked into the Commodore Room, where all the students would gather at the union, my reaction was physical: dry mouth, suddenly blurred vision as if something had jerked my head back, sweaty palms, a numb, frozen awkwardness to my body. I wanted only to flee, to get away, and I avoided the Commodore Room and other places like it. It was a behavioral pattern that went all the way back to at least when I was nine or ten years old.

Since I couldn't avoid those situations at Bread Loaf that jarred me in that terrifying way, I anaesthetized myself, just as I'd been doing for years. I drank. All the way through high school, in order to be popular and witty and a good dancer, I drank. During our four summers there in those beautiful, heavily wooded mountains, while Loretta worked on her master's degree (which she was awarded—from Middlebury College—in the summer of 1972), I drank more and more with each passing year, keeping a buzz all summer long. We were living in a little log cabin on top of a hill in the Green Mountain National Forest (the very same cabin where John Berryman had written many of *The Dream Songs* a few years before), and I would start drinking in the mornings when Loretta would leave to drive down to the Bread Loaf campus. Bread Loaf was a very sociable place, with lots of drinking and partying; we rented from Dulcie Scott, the Grande Dame of Bread Loaf, who had many cocktail parties on the porch of her rambling summer house, and just up the road from our cabin was the ski lodge of the poet William Meredith, who became a drinking buddy and later a lifelong, dear friend and our daughter's godfather.

On the drive up to Bennington from Williamstown the next day, I stopped at a liquor store and bought several bottles of Scotch, some bourbon, and a quart of vodka. I knew, if I was going to be drinking, I'd need a snort some mornings to get going and vodka, supposedly, could not be smelled on your breath. I don't know why it mattered. I knew nobody but Gardner, and I knew he wouldn't have noticed if I was snockered out of my mind. I got registered and settled in one of the residence cottages; I hurried through the registration process so I wouldn't have to talk to people. I didn't make friends easily, and from the start on that lovely campus I felt the old familiar sensation of odd man out. I was forty years old, slightly older than most of the other workshop participants, and

I could not believe that any of them wanted especially to befriend me or even talk to me. I was a Southerner, with a pronounced drawl that in my earlier times in New England rarely failed to draw a comment, and that made me self-conscious.

In my room I had a couple of quick drinks—sitting, looking out the window, feeling the soft sweet breeze off the mountain, while I felt my brain and my body relaxing and calming—then walked up to the student gathering place in the middle of the campus, the Svaha Café, a place that had short orders, wine and beer, several billiard tables, and a jukebox. I saw John Gardner there, holding forth at a table laden with empty beer bottles; he greeted me warmly.

It was my kind of place: a campus with a student union that sold wine and beer. I knew I'd be okay; I'd never be too far away from a drink of some kind. I could manage this. Nick Delbanco was young, handsome, booted, and I was assigned to his workshop. He was extremely nice, as gentle and polite as Gardner was terse. My workshop group seemed friendly and welcoming; one of the attractive younger women told me flirtily that she'd thought at first I was one of the teachers. I set up a schedule of conferences with Gardner to work with him one to one on revising my novel. I sipped my liquor, and I made friends. Everyone there was like-minded, worshiping the written word. It was an exhilarating experience, always under a satisfying cloak of respect for fiction, for all literature. Bernard Malamud lived just off campus, and one of the visiting writers was John Cheever, who liked and praised one of my stories. ("Somewhere in All This Green." It was chosen by Delbanco and Gardner to appear in an anthology of Bennington writers, and it was later the title story to my collection *Somewhere in All This Green: New and Selected Stories.*) I indulged in all-night poker sessions and shot pool at the Svaha. There were bull sessions, long conversations about writing and literature, and I flirted with all the pretty girls. I smoked dope with some of the younger writers. I had a good time and I learned a great deal about fiction writing.

But Gardner and I didn't make much progress on my novel. He

was very heavy into a new girlfriend, who was often in his office when I'd show up, sitting in his lap, reading his mail to him. Gardner roared around the narrow mountain roads on his motorcycle, his long blond hair flapping out behind him from beneath his helmet, usually with Liz, his girlfriend, perched on the back. We spent long hours around a table in the Svaha. We shot pool with a young black scholarship student from Manhattan. Gardner wasn't any better a pool player than I was. He was a free spirit and I liked him very much and was grateful to him for what he did teach me about fiction writing. When he was killed in a motorcycle accident some years later, American letters lost a unique one.

There was to be a big party, a barbeque, on the last day. I didn't feel like facing that, so I just left. I packed up my car in the dead of night and left about four in the morning, before daylight. I didn't tell a soul I was leaving. It was over and I wanted to just get away, even though I'd liked the experience. But I knew it was largely wasted because of my drinking. One more thing thrown away in a lifetime of them. But what the hell.

I left with a plastic cup of vodka in the cup holder of the TR-7. The vodka would get me home. I spent one night on the road, at a Motel 6 in Knoxville. I tried to cut down on my drinking, so I wouldn't be so wiped out when I got home, so I didn't sleep very much. Loretta was waiting for me; she had carried Meredith over to Patti Marxsen's house. I was home, back on my own turf. I was happy to see her; she made me feel complete again. We made love.

Three

On a warm, rainy day in the summer of 1955, I was rolling around in the mud behind the shrubbery outside the Webbs' lake cottage just off Highway 43 south of Demopolis. I was a senior in high school and I was with a girl named Ellen, who was from Florence in North Alabama, visiting for the summer. She was unrestrained and wicked. She had a trim, almost muscular figure, good boobs, and long tanned legs. She could drink most people under the table and her language would make a soldier blush.

During this summer a bunch of us had taken to going out to the lake house and partying all day and sometimes all night, too. Biboo Webb, one of my classmates whose family owned the lake house, would probably have gotten into serious trouble if we'd been discovered. Ellen was drunk that day, and she'd performed for us earlier. She was wearing skimpy, extremely tight short shorts, and she had straddled the chair in which my cousin Bob was sitting, her crotch right in front of his face. She said in a singsongy voice, "Keep a cool tool, fool, I'm wise to that rise in your Levi's." Everybody had thought that was pretty funny, especially considering the silly grin plastered on Bob's face.

The party had gone on all day. People, coming and going, had gotten stuck on the dirt and gravel road leading to the cabin. Drunken groups of us would go out in the driving rain to push the cars out, getting thoroughly wetted through and covered with black mud. It was an orgy of booze and half-dressed teenagers, trying to dry their clothes.

That party, that crowd, reflected the culture in which I grew up. Camaraderie and friendship, hard drinking, the generosity of one to another, trust, and the belief that Yes, there is a tomorrow, but it doesn't really matter because we are privileged and life is working well for us, we are in the good plan. We were young white people, it was the fifties, a time when there was no war, no depression, just black music for our pleasure and edification. We did not hate black people; ours was more a sin of indifference. We lived in a totally segregated society, but we were blind to most of the injustices in the world. What could go wrong with our lives? We were the center of the universe, and most of our lives were already mapped out and we were going on automatic pilot. Everybody knew what the future held: universities, fraternities and sororities, marriage, good jobs. Everybody but me. I didn't know who the hell I was nor where I was going. But I went along with the group as though I did.

Demopolis was a unique town in which to grow up. It was founded in 1817 by exiles from the court of Napoleon Bonaparte and seemed to have been invested from the start by a kind of sophistication that did not exist in surrounding communities. Demopolites were snobs; we were likely to scathingly refer to the inhabitants of Linden, the county seat, as being from "below the bogue," a reference to Chickasaw Bogue Creek, a small stream that cut across the southernmost section of the county. "Oh, well, you know he's from 'below the bogue,'" was all the explanation needed in assessing the crudity and perceived lack of class of certain people.

The culture I was raised in was a hard-drinking one. All our parents visited back and forth in each other's homes, and the greeting at the door was always "Can I get you a drink?" "A drink" usually meant bourbon and water, though there were occasional Scotch and gin drinkers, the gin likely in a Tom Collins or other such drink, never martinis. It was all very convivial, and it was only natural that teens coming along, adopting their own social bearings, would ape that behavior. It was a culture where drinking, sometimes abusive drinking, was not only accepted but expected and even encouraged.

There were three women's social clubs in town; each one held a huge formal dance each year, either at the community house or at the Elks Club downtown. The Silhouettes, the most exclusive, made up of the wealthiest matrons, held the most coveted date: New Year's Eve. They were all lavish black-tie affairs, with an orchestra and a lead-out, culminating with an early-morning breakfast in the dining room of the Demopolis Inn. The amount of liquor consumed was legendary. It gushed like water out of an artesian well.

Naturally, the teenaged girls in town—in imitation—had their own exclusive club, or sorority: the DTDs. The girls were sworn to secrecy and would not reveal what the initials of the club stood for. An invitation to join the DTDs was a coming out; only the most popular and pretty girls made the membership list. If you were poor and didn't wear stylish clothes, you could forget it. They held a dance every year and a progressive supper on Thanksgiving. In their initiation rites each year, young girls were run down Washington Street, smeared with lipstick, clothed in rags, with the members riding in open cars berating them, yelling at them, to the amusement of people on the street who came out of the stores to watch the spectacle go by. It was whispered about that the girls held an even more bizarre ceremony at some undisclosed location where unspeakable acts of a vaguely sexual nature were performed, an illusion that the girls did little to dispel. They greatly enjoyed the attention and the hint of naughty scandal. Their dances, too, were heavy-drinking affairs, and the first stop of the progressive supper was always cocktails at some girl's house.

Of course, if you were a teenaged boy, you had to be invited to these affairs by one of the girls. If you were dating one of them, you had no problem. The club always issued a number of "stag" invitations every year, so I usually got to go to the dance, though only one time did I have a date, a girl with whom I otherwise never would have wanted to go out. And I never went to the progressive supper. It was a big deal in town, who got invited and who didn't. It bothered me when I didn't get invited, but I usually had to work anyway. Sometimes, when I did go as a stag, I was too shy to break in on the beautiful couples. Unless, of course, I was drunk, in which case I was charming as all hell and danced with the best of them. I think, looking back, I was even then bothered by the "elitist" nature of these clubs, especially the DTDs. But I was still too insecure to figure out that I was right to be troubled. It was just one more thing, one more attitude, that separated me from the world around me, and I believed, of course, that the fault was mine. I was an oddball.

When I was nine or ten years old, I went over to the old Cobb place in Sumter County to spend a week one summer with my Uncle Russell and his family. Uncle Russell was the first alcoholic I'd ever known up close. He was my father's younger brother, who had agreed to live on the cattle farm and take care of my grandfather until he died. He ran a little country store and gristmill out in front of the house. Uncle Russ continued to run the operation until his own death by acute alcohol poisoning.

I would play with the young black boys, riding mules and fishing in the creek. I'd ride around the place with Uncle Russ in his pickup. We'd stop at various wells and my uncle would take out a pint of whiskey, ask me to get him a dipper of water for a chaser, and take a snort from the bottle. This went on all day. When my whole family would go over to the home place for Sunday dinner, even before my grandfather died, my father and Uncle Russ would go out to the "store" for an hour or two before lunch and have drinks. Uncle Russ would sit there at the dinner table with a lopsided, snaggled grin (he was losing his teeth), not saying much. Aunt Frances and my two girl cousins, along with my parents, just ignored him. But I couldn't. I looked with a fascination that I did not understand. The image of that grin, the incongruous nature of it, has vividly remained with me all these years. After dinner I might pass through one of the back bedrooms and Uncle Russ would be sprawled on the bed, sound asleep, his mouth gaping open, an afternoon breeze stirring the curtains.

My father wouldn't have the telltale grin at the table, and that was a mystery to me until I was much older and figured out that, unlike my father, Uncle Russ had been drinking since he'd first gotten up that morning. I still feel connected to him. We are more than kin.

Four

I was born on October 20, 1937, in the back bedroom of a rented wood frame house on a dusty dirt street in the little village of Eutaw, in Greene County, Alabama. My parents had dropped out of Livingston State Teachers College to marry; neither ever completed a degree. My father worked at Sumter Farm and Stock Company. It was in the depths of the Great Depression, and it must have been difficult for my father to be a clerk in a general store with a young family to feed and house.

When I was six months old, my father took a job with Sheffield Truck and Tractor Company in Demopolis, a bigger town twenty miles to the south, on the Tombigbee River in Marengo County. We moved and lived in two rooms at the back of a large two-story antebellum house on North Main Street. My father was a parts man at Sheffield's, a much better paying job than the one he'd had. We soon had a rental house, a small wooden cottage at the corner of Commissioners and West Perry Streets. There is a picture of me when I was not yet two years old in front of that house, sitting on the seat with Jim, an old Negro man, in his Billy goat wagon. He took the wagon up and down the streets, many of which were still unpaved, and children all over town would take rides with him. (Much later, after I was a professor of English at Montevallo, the picture was reprinted on the front page of *The Demopolis Times* with the following caption: "Pictured is Billy Cobb, now a professor at Alabama College, with Jim and his Billy goat wagon, circa 1939. The maid's name was not remembered." Standing in the background is a tall, lean, handsome black woman who was obviously my "nurse," as they were called.)

My father's family lived on a sizable cattle farm outside Livingston, in Sumter County, near Boyd, the selfsame place that my Uncle Russ would later run. By the time I was born, my paternal grandmother, Iva Elizabeth Nunnery Cobb, was dead, having succumbed to breast cancer in 1933. The old home place, a large, rambling two-story house with porches around three sides, burned down a few years after her death. There were five children in the family, three boys and two girls, of which my father was the middle. My grandfather, William Francis Cobb, "Mr. Will," built a small white frame house in the same location, where he lived until he died shortly after World War II. The tiny general store in front of the house, called "Cobb's Trading Post," had a gristmill and two old hand-pumped gas tanks.

My mother's family was from Gilbertown, in the red clay hills of Choctaw County, down in Southwest Alabama. They were the Lands. Glenn Land, Sr., my grandfather, was the postmaster and rural mail carrier. He traded mules and also had a large patch of corn. Beyond the mule lot and the cornfield, in some scrub woods, was a large mule-pulled mill that I only in later years realized was the first step in making corn whiskey, white lightning, a product for which Choctaw County was famous. I don't think my grandfather was a moonshiner by trade, but only made small amounts for his own use, and by the time I was old enough to know what whiskey was, my grandfather was drinking bottled, bonded whiskey which my father bought and carried to him, since Choctaw was a dry county. My mother called it "Pa-Pa's medicine." My grandmother was a Martin from Rose Hill, Mississippi. There were two boys and three girls, my mother the second to the youngest. She was called "Sissy" in the family, and was the only sibling to go to college.

My parents' first house burned to the ground one raw winter night. I must have been close to two years old then, and I have a dim memory of the fire, of the acrid bitter smell of the smoke and the chaos of tall, big men moving furniture out into the front yard. There followed then my first truly vivid memory: I was being carried in someone's arms, presumably my father's, into a house with large vacant rooms, no furniture, only echoes of footsteps, a place where all life had been removed.

That house was my parents' second rental house, and the one we lived in until they built their own house when I was in the sixth grade. The house is still there, looking much the same as it did around 1940. It was a small brick bungalow with a screen porch on the front, on North Commissioners Street, directly across the street from Bluff Hall, an imposing antebellum mansion perched atop the high white chalk bluffs of the Tombigbee. There were three bedrooms and one bathroom shotgunned on one side of the house: a guest room in the front, my parents' bedroom in the middle, and mine—and very soon my sister's—in the rear. A narrow driveway paved with ashes—never used—ran down that side of the house to a leaning tin garage in the rear that was used as a storage shed and a coal bin. The house was heated by coal fireplaces and a small coal stove in the kitchen, a room at the back opposite my bedroom. The other two rooms were a dining room in the middle and a living room at the front. The small bathroom had a claw-foot tub.

A back fence covered with privet and wild honeysuckle vines overlooked an empty concrete swimming pool behind Trinity Episcopal Church, which faced Main Street on the eastern side of the block. Against this fence, in our backyard, was an empty chicken yard. There was a chinaberry tree and two small peach trees and a huge fruit-bearing fig tree against the house, which provided climbing opportunities for a boy and his friends, often serving as a big imaginary World War II bomber. It also kept us in fig preserves.

My sister, Jayne Elizabeth Cobb, was born when I was two and a half years old. We shared the back bedroom until we moved to the new house on South Main Street in 1949. My father went to work every morning at 6 a.m., returned to the house about eight for breakfast, then went back. He came home to lunch every day. Sheffield's was only three blocks away, on Washington Street, near downtown. My mother did not work outside the home until Jayne and I were both in high school, when she went to work as a clerk at Frohsin's Department Store. We both had "nurses," black women who spent the day with us, pushing Jayne in her stroller to the city park, with its swings and creaky wooden merry-go-round, while I tagged along. On nice days there would be forty or fifty "nurses," with their charges, in the park. I learned to play with other children there, while the "nurses" visited in groups in the shade around the goldfish pond in the middle of the square.

About this time I acquired my first pet: a piglet. We often went over to my grandfather's farm for visits, for Sunday dinner, sometimes with some of my aunts and uncles and cousins, sometimes just our family. There was a hog pen in the backyard, next to a windmill, and on one of our visits there were several new piglets. I asked my grandfather if I could have one. He said I could, but I would have to go out and catch me one. He knew I couldn't catch one, and I knew it, too, so I asked the cook Punchy's son Frank, about ten years old, to catch one for me, which he did. My grandfather was flabbergasted when I came in with the little pink pig, but he had promised it to me so he gave it to me, over my mother's objections and to the great amusement of my father and my Uncle Russell, who had already been out to the "store" for a few snorts.

My father constructed a pen for the pig in the chicken yard out back and we fed it scraps from the table. I was not allowed to let the pig out, so I had to just watch him in the pen. The pig soon grew into a hog. When he got big enough, he would root under the fence and get out, and Jayne and I would delight in playing with him in the backyard. We could not get the pig to stay in the pen, and he would wander around the neighborhood. Everybody knew whose pig it was.

One day my mother, who was something of a priss, was walking downtown to go shopping, when she met the pig coming home. I can envision her on the sidewalk: a pretty, dark-haired woman, little more than a girl, an "afternoon dress," high heels, a cigarette holder that she affected for as long as she smoked. The pig turned and headed back to town with her, heeling like a dog. He followed her all over town. My mother was so embarrassed by the incident that she made my father promise to get rid the animal. He gave it to a farmer he knew, who butchered the hog and gave us back a ham and some bacon. My mother tried to cook some of the meat and serve it, but none of us could bear to eat our pig. She finally threw it all out.

My childhood was for the most part a happy one. The city pool and community house were a block away, and the river was just across the street. Demopolis is located at the confluence of the Tombigbee and the Black Warrior Rivers. The Black Warrior comes down from north of Birmingham, through Tuscaloosa (Creek for Black Warrior) to join the Tombigbee just northeast of the town, so that Demopolis is surrounded on three sides by water. The rivers provided a natural amusement park for boys (climbing on the bluffs, against my mother's stern orders; swimming in the swift currents, ditto; finding fool's gold—nuggets of pyrite—in the lime rock; rowing in "borrowed" skiffs), and the pool was a huge, Olympic-size, with a high wooden diving board on two levels. I went barefoot all summer long, grew tan from the sun. The winters were unusually cold, with several deep snows during the war years. Or at least in the pictures they looked deep, but our legs were so short that it was probably only a few inches. We would dress every morning in the kitchen. When we got up, we ran through the cold house to where my mother had our clothes hanging on chairs next to the coal stove, and shivering, we got into the warm clothes as quickly as possible. The kitchen was the only room in the house that was heated until up in the day, when my mother would build coal fires in the grates in the living room and the dining room. My job, when I got big enough, was to bring in the full coal scuttles from the bin out back.

The French émigrés who settled Demopolis early in the nineteenth century intended to grow grapes and olive trees, since they'd been told that the climate in that section of the old Mississippi Territory was similar to the one in Provence. The colony barely lasted the first winter. When I was a boy, there were still stunted olive trees growing here and there, and I knew where every one of them was. They bore a hard, inedible fruit that made wonderful ammunition for a slingshot. In the 1940s, there was still some French influence in the town, with examples of New Orleans–type architecture scattered in the downtown area, and there were still families with names like Moneir and Funeir. My friend Winston Smith later wrote extensively about The Vine and Olive Colony, as they were called, and it is a fascinating, if little known, chapter in Alabama history.

I'm certain that it was during the war years and shortly thereafter when I was shaped into a writer. I actually remember December 7, 1941; I didn't understand what was going on, but I knew something big was. My parents sent Jayne and me out to play in the backyard and told us to be quiet while they listened to the radio. It was unusual that they listened to the radio in the daytime, so I knew that something important was afoot.

The war would come home to us when, on some nights, planes from Craig Field over in Selma would fly over the town and we had to douse all the lights, even putting a blanket in front of the grates. My father, who was 4-F because of a bad back, was in the civilian defense corps, and he would go out and patrol on those nights, while we huddled in the living room listening to the planes drone overhead. I was frightened, since I was not absolutely sure those planes weren't German or Japanese ones. I can't imagine why anybody thought the enemy might come over and bomb Demopolis, but we took the drills very seriously.

My mother sent me, and in a year or two Jayne, to a kindergarten a block away from the house, up on Main Street, across from the Episcopal Church. It was run by a little old lady named Julia Lipscomb, who was the daughter of an officer in the Confederate army, Captain James Taylor Jones, who had a memorial window in the church. She was a widow, and everyone called her Miss Julia—the children, their parents, people in the town, everybody. Most of the middle-class children in town—the sons and daughters of working men like my father, of merchants, of professional men, of gentlemen farmers—went to the school, which Miss Julia called Northside Progressive School. A misnomer if there ever was one.

The school was held in the front rooms and side yard of her "cottage," a rambling antebellum house with wisteria and smilax growing across the front and side porches. I don't remember many specifics of the curriculum, though she must have taught us *something*— my friend Jerre Levy, who was in my class all the way through until high school graduation and was a professor of neuroscience at the University of Chicago before her retirement, told me that when we got to elementary school, in the first grade, I was in the "Blue Birds," the advanced reading group, along with her and Alan Koch, who later pitched in the major leagues with the Washington Senators, and Lester Crawford, who would be Director of the Food and Drug Administration under President George W. Bush.

I do remember that in the mornings we would sometimes, at least once a week, gather on the shaded side porch where Miss Julia had the flag of the Confederacy hanging on the wall, and she would lead us in the singing of "The Bonnie Blue Flag" while another elderly lady, Miss Lillian Batelle, pounded away on a piano inside in the parlor. "Hurrah, hurrah, for Southern rights hurrah, / Hurrah for the bonnie blue flag that bears a single star." We sang it all the way through. Much later, when I was in graduate school at Vanderbilt University, I endeared myself to my major professor, Donald Davidson, by knowing all the words to the song as he played it on a piano at a party and I sang with him.

And every spring there was a ceremony when all the children in the school would march en mass the two blocks to the town square, where there was a statue of a Confederate soldier. We would play on rudimentary instruments (tambourines, triangles, small drums) and sing "Dixie" while Miss Julia laid a wreath on the statue. All the mothers and fathers would come out of the stores downtown to watch us. Years later, my first major publication would be "The Stone Soldier," a short story that appeared in *Story* magazine and won their best of the year award. It would be collected in multiple anthologies and appears in my short story collection *Somewhere in All This Green.* The story is about that statue. Iva Ward Hammond, one of the main characters, is based loosely on Miss Julia, and Iva Ward Hammond's house is Miss Julia's house.

Every Christmas, Miss Julia would lead us back, holding hands, into the bowels of that rambling "cottage," to a back room where her ancient bedridden mother lived. The old woman was the widow of Captain Jones. She lay propped up in a four-poster bed, on yellowed pillows, a knitted fascinator on her head, and she peered down at us as we gathered around her bed to sing "Silent Night." We were all terrified. When we had finished our song, we filed by, holding our sweaty little hands up, and she placed in the palms her Christmas gift to each of us: one pecan.

That I stood there and looked into the eyes of a woman who had been married to a Confederate officer, who had borne his child, is astonishing to me as I look back. In that moment history was telescoped for me, and though I was not consciously aware of it at the time, I was embedded in the past, firmly attached to a dark time that, no matter how hard I would try, I would never be able to shake off. William Faulkner famously said that "the past is not past." I clearly remember the first time I read his great novel *Absalom, Absalom* when I was in college, and its story, its themes and nuances, were crystal clear to me. Faulkner was writing my own history. I felt and experienced the novel as if I had lived it, which is a testament to Faulkner's great genius; it is also an attestation that my history is Quentin Compson's history and the South's history is my own.

When I was in fourth grade, I had rheumatic fever, at that time a very serious disease. I was bedridden for seven months and missed most of the year of school. I was moved from the back bedroom into my parents' big double bed, and they moved into the guest room. I can recall many days when I tossed and turned with the fever, the sweat pouring from my face, and I was later told that there were times when the doctor didn't think I would make it. I was intensely sick for a month or two. There followed a long convalescence, when I was not allowed to get out of bed except to go to the bathroom.

My fourth grade teacher—I remember her name was Mrs. Martin—sent work home for me by Jayne, who was in the second grade. I listened to the radio a lot, shows like *The Shadow*, *The Green Hornet*, and one I particularly liked, *Bobby Benson and the B Bar B Riders*. Every day at noon I listened to a comedy show called *The Duke of Paducah*. He would say repeatedly, to my great amusement, "I'm goin' back to the wagon, boys, these shoes are killin' me!" I began to read. I read every book in the house, and my mother would get me books from the public library in the town square. I read all the Hardy Boys books, *Treasure Island*, *The Swiss Family Robinson*, and Robert Louis Stevenson's *A Child's Garden of Verse*. I devoured comic books; every kid in the neighborhood sent me theirs as soon as they finished them.

One friend, Winston Smith, who lived several blocks away in

another section of town, had the entire collection of The Wizard of Oz books, the large-format editions with the full-color illustrations. He let me borrow them, and I loved them. I became addicted to reading—my first addiction, I suppose. I loved escaping into other worlds. I must have wanted, even that early, to create them myself. I wrote a two-page "novel," which my mother kept for years before it got thrown away. I wrote a poem that won a prize on the local radio station and was read over the air. The first prize was a free ticket to the movies at the Marengo Theater, but of course, I couldn't go. Still, it was my first literary endeavor, my first honor, the first recognition I received. During that illness and recovery, I became—for better or worse—an intense, habitual reader of fiction, and I have maintained that devotion my entire life. I discovered early on that the world is terrible and frightening as well as beautiful, and books made the world easier to navigate.

The bout with rheumatic fever left me with a heart murmur, which has never amounted to much other than getting me excused from PE when I was a freshman in college. I think it's gone now, though over the years I've had an occasional doctor tell me he could detect it. I was able to move on into the fifth grade with the rest of my class.

Winston Smith and I shared a close friendship that lasted until Winston's unfortunately early death after we were both professors of English, he at the University of Alabama and me at Montevallo. He lived a few blocks from me, on the northern edge of town. Between his house and the river was Mr. Carl Michael's pasture, with woods, streams, a couple of ponds, and meadows. We had all the areas of the pasture named, names we must have gotten from movies or our reading: the San Fernando Valley, Lookout Mountain, the Great Lakes. We had a clubhouse in a room over his parents' garage and played together almost every day. He was a grade ahead of me in school, but we were about the same age, and we were best friends all the way through graduate school at Vanderbilt, where we shared an apartment in Nashville one year. He was a fine poet.

He had compiled a collection of his poems called *Summer Talk*, but in spite of my urging, he would never submit any of his poems for publication nor show them to anybody else.

One incident from that period of my childhood is burned into my memory. The people next door had a pony they kept in a pen in their backyard. Their fence ran along the side of our house and on the edge of our backyard. The pony was handsome. It was bigger than a Shetland pony, the size of a small horse. And it was insane. It would gallop around the pen shaking its head in a bizarre fashion; nobody ever rode the pony or played with it or, as I remember, paid any attention to it at all. It was just always there. Naturally I was fascinated with it. I watched it and fed it through the fence. When I'd come into the backyard, the pony would come galloping, whinnying. I guess I imagined that we were friends.

My sister was having a birthday party in the spring of the year after my fever. All the kids were playing in the backyard. I was Big Brother, and I wanted to impress them all and show them the pony, so I climbed the fence. I had an apple for the pony. I held it out to him. I heard the kids screaming, and before I knew what was happening, I was on the ground. The pony had butted me in the chest and knocked me backward. He bit a chunk out of the skin on my chest and reared up and kicked me in the mouth with one of his hooves. I remember looking up and seeing the pony over me, the wild look in his eyes, his bared teeth. Suddenly he wheeled and was gone. The children were all crying and screaming, especially Jayne, and my mother came running. I scrambled back over the fence. I must have been in a state of shock, blood running down my chin, my shirt ripped up the front and bloody, but I was safe. The pony was galloping around and around the pen like some maniacal dervish.

I saw clearly then what had made the pony run away from me. Standing in front of the group of excited and frightened children, mostly girls, was a boy slightly larger than the rest. He had a handful of rocks and was still pelting the pony with them as it ran. I don't know if I knew it then, or if anybody did really, but I realized it later and I know it now. He saved me from being badly hurt, maybe even saved my life. He had the presence of mind to start throwing rocks at the mad pony when he attacked me. He was a mentally challenged boy from out in the country, my sister's age, Kervin Brasfield. I have thanked him, but now I do so publicly: Thank you, Kervin, for being the one who thought quickly enough to save me that day.

My teacher in the sixth grade was the principal of the elementary school, Doc Knight. Mr. Knight brought Little League baseball to Demopolis, and I played the first year on one of the first teams organized in town. Doc Knight was the first in a long line of teachers and coaches who were role models and father figures for me. He encouraged me and took time with me. I suppose he is responsible for my lifelong love of baseball. (He appears as Doc Day in my baseball story "The Night of the Yellow Butterflies.")

My baseball career did not begin auspiciously. My age group was the oldest eligible for Little League, so we got to play only one year. Doc organized Babe Ruth League, the next level, where I was able to play two years. The year in Little League, when I played for Braswell Brothers Hardware, I did not get a hit the entire season. I must have set a record for strikeouts. I was a second baseman, pretty good in the field, but I stank up the batter's box.

It was during those years, for several consecutive summers, that my parents sent me to Camp Grist, a YMCA camp over near Selma. It was a two-week camp. Paul Grist was a middle-aged jock with a crew cut, surrounded by clones from high school and college. Everybody was supposed to worship him and his crew. Since I didn't, I assumed something was terribly wrong with me. I thought many of the activities had a cruel and sadistic undertone. I remember one practice when the new boys were made to kneel before a roaring campfire and bow, repeating after a counselor, "O, Wat-a, Goo, Siam." Once you realized what you were saying, you could get up and whisper it to a counselor. The boys who didn't get it would have to keep repeating it, moving closer and closer to the fire. There were always one or two boys who took forever, and were getting their eyebrows singed, before they figured it out, to the howling amusement of all the other boys and the counselors. Even though I quickly figured it out, I hated it and refused to participate again. I was given demerits and forced to do extra duty washing pans and dishes in the dining hall.

I was very modest and self-conscious. I did not like the communal showers. I was so ashamed of the odors I made taking a shit that I'd wait until the other boys were engaged in something else before I went to the latrine. I was lousy at all the sports; I couldn't swim fast or run fast, and once when coaxed into boxing, an older taller boy knocked me on my ass, to everyone's enormous entertainment. I never won a ribbon. I think I was the only boy in the entire camp who didn't (some had piles of them), and I would skip activities and stay in the cabin in my bunk and pray that I'd win one. I'd feel sorry for myself. It was the first time, though certainly not the last, when I felt like an outcast. I spent a lot of time alone.

Once, when I was at Camp Grist, after Little League and before I began to play Babe Ruth League, Jayne sent me a short article she had clipped out of a *Weekly Reader* or somewhere. It was tips on hitting by Ted Williams. One of the things he said was "Keep your eye on the ball." I realized with a jolt that that's what I hadn't been doing. When I swung, I took my eye off the ball. Something as simple as that. I'm sure I'd been told before to keep my eye on the ball, but I'd never really known what they were talking about. Ted Williams suggested you watch the ball all the way from the pitcher's hand until it hit your bat.

I was on Sheffield's team, along with Alan Koch. Some years before, our fathers, along with two other men, had bought out Sheffield's Truck and Tractor Company and moved it from downtown out onto Highway 80. My father was the general manager and Alan's father was the CFO. In our practices Alan pitched to me. He was already a tall boy and was developing into a very good pitcher. Not many boys in the league could hit his pitches, but I began to hit line drives off him. All of a sudden, thanks to Ted Williams and my darling sister, Jayne, I was a hitter.

I was a leadoff man and played second base. Alan and I both made the all-star team that first year and played in the state tournament. The next year we again made the all-star team and were both starters. (I batted .420 that year.) We went all the way through the state tournament, beating Montgomery 11–2 in the championship, and went on to the regionals in Morristown, Tennessee, where we eventually lost to Natchez, Mississippi. Alan continued to develop as a pitcher, and I held my own. When we were seniors in high school, we won the state championship again, beating Woodlawn High School of Birmingham two out of three games at Rickwood Field. Alan pitched the two games we won. He would go on to pitch for Auburn University and then in the Big Leagues.

My father was now making pretty good money, and we built a new house on South Main Street near the elementary school. Jayne and I had our own rooms. We had left the little brick house on Commissioners Street and now lived in a nice new centrally heated three-bedroom house with white asbestos shingles that made my mother very happy.

Five

I was still fumbling my way through some understanding of sex. I liked the pornography I occasionally saw, pictures of sex acts on playing cards that I suppose some much older boy had brought back from the Army, and the well-thumbed little eight-page comics that were passed around. (Tijuana Bibles. We called them "fuck books.") I inspected these with an eager curiosity that surpassed any I had for my formal schoolwork. I purchased a copy of the very first issue of *Playboy*, with Marilyn Monroe on the cover, at Bailey's Drug Store downtown. I bought and read a copy every month, and of course looked at the pictures. I don't think my parents even knew what *Playboy* was and I wound up with an entire collection, stacked in the attic, which my mother threw away when I went off to college (along with my complete collection of baseball cards, including a Mickey Mantle rookie card, a development that I recognize is a real cliché, but in my case it was true). I even subscribed to *Playboy* for a while, along with *Sport Magazine* and *Outdoor Life*. My parents never seemed suspicious of my avid magazine reading, but back then there was not the plethora of skin magazines, *Hustler* and its cousins, that came along later. My father only raised his eyebrows and expressed disapproval when I brought home paperback editions of novels like *From Here to Eternity*. He equated paperback books with trash. He refused to believe that these were inexpensive reprints of good books that had been recently published in hardcover, no matter how much I tried to explain the concept to him.

My father and I had only one conversation about sex, if you could even call it a conversation. When I was about twelve or so, a movie came to town that was all hush hush, whisper whisper. It was about sex. An "educational" film. There would be two showings: an afternoon matinee for mothers and daughters and an evening showing for fathers and sons. My father asked me if I wanted to go, and of course I did. He was pretty solemn about it. I was in the bathtub and he was at the mirror shaving. We weren't talking, but of course where we were about to go was heavy in the air. Suddenly, he said, "Billy, you know what this picture's about, don't you?" He didn't look at me, just kept shaving. "Yes sir," I said. "Okay," he said, and nodded. And that was the totality of all the communication my father and I ever had on the subject.

I vividly remember standing in a line in the lobby, waiting to go in, when the women and girls came out. It was both awkward and titillating. It was a small town, and we all knew each other—some of the girls were giggling, boldly looking into our eyes; others were shy, eyes downcast. What is astonishing to me, looking back, is that there was not a word exchanged between the two groups. The movie was terrible, about some girl who gets pregnant; there was a lot of talk, no nudity, no sex, a big disappointment.

So my "education" about sex was extremely fucked up. I tacitly learned that it was something not to be discussed, except with other boys, usually older ones who instructed me with odd, confused, even bizarre information. My mother, in front of me, in conversation with one of her friends, said of another woman, "Yes, she's p-r-e-g," spelling it out so, I suppose, I wouldn't hear the word *pregnant*. Or maybe back then you didn't use that word even with other women, I don't know. There must have been thousands of examples like that, hammering away at my young mind, shaping my thoughts.

It was along about the eighth grade, when I was in junior high school, that I discovered *The Catcher in the Rye* in the high school library. I was overwhelmed by the novel. I passed it along to a good friend who loved to read as much as I did: Lester Crawford. We recommended it to others. When more and more people started reading it, the administration got suspicious. It was not at all usual for large numbers of Demopolis junior high kids to be excited by reading *novels*. Some irate parents got involved, and the book was soon withdrawn from circulation. The sweet little lady who ran the library pled that when she ordered it, she had thought it was a baseball book. Her name was Mrs. Probst. One day after all the hoopla had died down, I was reading in the library and I looked up and she was looking at me from her desk. She gave me a huge wink. I read *From Here to Eternity* then, too. I was reading just about anything I could get my hands on. I clearly remember a book that Lester Crawford found and brought to school for me to read called *The Werewolf of Paris*. It was weird and very sexy and we both loved it. We thought it was funny as hell.

Lester Crawford was becoming a good friend. He would be one of my closest friends during high school. We later roomed together at Auburn when I went there as a freshman, and later still I was in his wedding in Birmingham. After the reception, which was quite a party (Lester married into a wealthy family), everyone was paired off but me. I couldn't find anyone to continue drinking with, so I wound up getting very drunk all by myself in the apartment where Lester had arranged for the groomsmen to stay. I woke up in the morning very hung over and left without speaking to anyone. Lester and his bride lived in Auburn, and I was living in Nashville at the time. I didn't see him again for many years, but we spoke on the phone occasionally.

Lester was brilliant, but unorthodox. Lester's father owned a farm out near Gallion, and we spent much time together during those formative years. He got a degree in veterinary medicine at Auburn, then a PhD from the University of Georgia. He went to work for the FDA in Washington and eventually rose to be its head.

For as long as I could remember, my parents had hauled me off every Sunday morning to Sunday school and church. The Cobbs were staunch Presbyterians (my mother had been raised in a little country Methodist church, but she became a Presbyterian when they were married). I say "hauled me off," because I never really wanted to go. Everything we talked about on Sunday mornings had absolutely nothing to do with my life the other six days of the week. It just never made a whole lot of sense to me and I kept Jesus, the draggy hymns, the boring sermons, the interminable pastoral prayers and all the rest neatly compartmentalized to Sunday mornings and didn't let them interfere with the rest of my world. My father lived to be ninety-three years of age, and in all that time we never had one single serious conversation about religion. I had many questions early on, but I soon learned that you simply didn't express any doubts. You kept your mouth shut and waited until Monday, when it would all go away. That was the primary thing I learned about the stoic Southern Presbyterian way.

I remember going to the Sunday school in a little frame wood cottage out behind the church, where we played in sandboxes building replicas of scenes in the Holy Land and heard stories from the Bible. We had little carved puppets we dressed in scraps of cloth to look like the Biblical people we saw in the illustrations. It was fun, even interesting, but I recall being puzzled about the significance of it all. It seemed endowed with some deeper import that was never explained to me to my satisfaction. It was *different* from what we learned in regular school. It was a mystery—of course it was—but what was baffling to me even as a small child was that the other kids in the class and the adults supervising the classes did not seem to find it mysterious at all.

The church did not prepare me for the things I was discovering in life. Quite the contrary. It reemphasized my feelings of isolation. First Presbyterian in Demopolis was a gray stone church as cold and joyless inside as it looked from the outside. None of my friends went there. My cousins Mitch and Linda Cobb and Bob Reeves attended, but at that time we were not close. It seemed to me that the people who went to the Presbyterian Church were misfits. I certainly felt like one. (Other kids often asked me, "What do Presbyterians *believe*?" I had no idea what to tell them.) All of this further contributed to my feelings of never quite fitting in, and they weren't helped when I was sent to the Methodist Church every summer for Daily Vacation Bible School, since we had so few children we had to hook up with them. All the Methodist children were cliquish and seemed to have some common understanding that was forever closed off from me.

I think this may have been part of the reason I failed so miserably in the Boy Scouts, in my short active period never rising above the rank of Tenderfoot. The meetings were held in the Methodist Church Sunday School building, and I had that same feeling of "odd ball out." It apparently didn't bother any of the other boys, many of whom were Baptists and other denominations. I know it bothered at least some of the Jewish boys, especially my friend Alan Koch, who was just as frustratingly attempting to "belong" as I was. Of course we never talked about those things. I suffered silently, feeling very alone. I enjoyed the out of doors, camping out, sleeping under the stars (Loretta and I continued to camp with Meredith through her adolescence) but I didn't like the organized, stratified orderliness of the Scouts. I couldn't seem to buy into the worshipful attitude toward badges, the oath, and all the rules of young manhood, which struck me as phony and unimportant.

I worked at various odd jobs from time to time. My parents paid me to mow the grass, and I worked out at Sheffield's some, helping with inventory and running errands. I got my first real job when I was fourteen, at the Marengo Theater. The manager of the

Marengo was Joyce McCluskey, who has remained a good friend. I loved movies, and I enjoyed my job immensely, since I got to see about every one that came to town, and for free. Some of them two or three times.

My main job became working in the colored balcony. The Marengo Theater was a much larger theater than was typical of the other small towns in the area. It had a large lobby, chandeliers, many colorful posters of coming attractions, deep carpets, and an auditorium that seated about five hundred people. It was, of course, segregated, and African-Americans sat in the balcony. The theater faced Washington Street, with a box office and recessed double doors set back from the sidewalk under a large marquee. Black people bought their tickets from a separate window around to the side, and there was a separate entrance with their own popcorn machine and candy counter off the main lobby. I loved working the balcony. It was one of the best jobs I ever had.

I had been going to the Marengo Theater since I was a toddler, walking to the movies on Saturdays when I got older. Before I began working there, my family would go every Sunday night; later, after I had worked Sunday afternoon and evening, I would go out to the car and sleep while my parents finished watching the movie. I remember going to the movies once after the incident with the pony, when I had a big white bandage on my lower lip. When I got home and looked in the mirror, I was astonished to see that the bandage was midnight black. I had been eating licorice sticks; nobody had said anything to me about it, but surely they noticed it.

Demopolis was awash with eccentric and colorful characters during my young years, and some of them were black people. One was Joe Bynymo. His real name was Armstead King, but everyone called him Joe Bynymo. He walked the streets of the town in a long black overcoat in the summertime and in shirtsleeves in the winter. He carried a bullwhip over his shoulder. He was fierce looking, with a cocked eye and a scar down the side of his face. The legend was that he had been walking along the riverbank one day when a wind came up and blew him across the river and rapped his head against a white oak tree, causing him to change his name to Joe Bynymo. Buddy Ed Logan, a black man with whom I worked at the Marengo, told me that that was a myth. "That ol' nigger got hit upside the head with a sawed-off pool cue, what happened," he said. (I wrote my second novel, *The Hermit King*, about Joe, and he also appears in a minor role in *A Walk Through Fire*.)

Another was an old man named Greensboro, who walked up and down the street beating on a bass drum. (He is in *The Hermit King* as well.) A third was a man from out at Salt Well who used to ride up and down the alleys in his mule-drawn wagon loaded with fresh vegetables, calling out "Old Man on his job, today! Selllllin' okry!" White ladies all over town would come out and buy from him in the backyards. My friend Jim Haskins later told me that his name was Pet-Jack.

There was much laughing and joking in the small lobby of the balcony. The black customers all called me "Mr. Billy," many of them in a half-joking manner that I didn't mind. I had always had black friends and playmates since the days when we lived up on Commissioners Street, when one of my friends was a boy named Henry Haskins. We played together often down along the river, later shooting basketballs together on a goal that my father put up in the backyard of the house on Main, until we were both in junior high school and went our separate ways.

Henry and I were good friends. Many years later, when I settled on the plot of my novel about the civil rights movement that became *A Walk Through Fire*, I based the character of Eldon Long, the black minister involved in voter registration drives in Hammond, the little town I modeled on Demopolis, on Henry. Our friendship suggested the one between Eldon and O. B. Brewster in the novel. We had lost touch and I had long since moved away from Demopolis, so I didn't really know what had happened in Henry's life. Imagine my surprise when I read a memoir by a white civil rights worker who was in Demopolis in the mid-sixties and discovered that the leader of the movement in Demopolis was a handsome black man named Henry Haskins. We later reconnected, mainly though Henry's younger brother Jim Haskins, who was a writer of some renown that I got to know through book fairs and writers conferences and visits with him in New York. Demopolis had a History and Heritage Festival in the late seventies, and they invited both Jim Haskins and me (along with Alan Koch, who was retired from his baseball career, had become an attorney and had written about the Jewish Heritage in the town). After we spoke, we had dinner together. Henry, who has since passed away, as has Jim, was there; he was minister of a large black Baptist church in Birmingham. It was almost as though I had instinctively known much of his life and career when I wrote the book.

I can also trace some other roots of that novel to this period. There was a very beautiful black girl who came to the movies often. She was stunning. I was fifteen; she was sixteen or seventeen, I imagine. Her figure made me gape and inflamed my already raging fantasies. She was flirtatious, witty, poised, and confident in ways that I assuredly was not. I was extremely attracted to her. She flirted with me openly. Sometimes, when I held out my hand to take her ticket, she raked her nails across my palm and smiled into my eyes. I had, of course, seen many attractive black women in the movies (Lena Horne and Dorothy Dandridge come to mind, two that she resembled), and with my mind as preoccupied with sex as it was, I had noticed lots of saucy black girls who came to the Marengo. But this one was something special, and I've never forgotten her. Her name was Rachel Rowser. Though we never actually did anything but flirt, I used my memories of Rachel when I created Cora and her relationship with the white O. B. Brewster in *A Walk Through Fire*. Years later, after I had given a reading from the novel at Miles College, a predominantly black school in Birmingham, an attractive young female faculty member rose from the audience and asked: "Mr. Cobb, is not your treatment of O. B.'s affair with Cora just another example of white male fantasies toward black women?"

I had an anxious moment when I thought, in something of a panic, that this might be Rachel Rowser, but she was just a little older than Rachel had been thirty-five years before. I stammered some quasi-literary answer, the kind of bullshit all writers learn to mumble when they are questioned about their work.

Ed Logan was the janitor at the Marengo. Everybody called him "Buddy Ed." (He appears in *The Hermit King*.) I worked several nights a week and all day on Saturdays, and Buddy Ed would sit in the balcony, talking and visiting with everybody. He was highly entertaining. His chatter was clever and funny. I could tell that he liked me, because I treated him with respect. Though I was very much a product of the Jim Crow South that I grew up in, I had no hostility toward black people. I was blind and insensitive, but my omissions of feeling were not malicious. I was actually more comfortable around my friends in the colored balcony than I was in some other situations more common in the world to which I belonged, the one on the other side of the divide.

I knew that Buddy Ed had observed my mutual flirtation with Rachel. He never mentioned it, but his eyes twinkled after she had passed through on her way up into the balcony. One day, on one of those occasions, I asked him, "Buddy Ed, would you fuck a white woman?"

He leaned back and smiled, nodding his head. "Mist Billy," he said, after a minute, "pussy ain't but pussy." One of the most profound things anybody ever said to me.

Six

Like most boys who grew up in the deep South, I hunted and fished. I was never much of a hunter (I never killed a deer) except for a period when I did a lot of bird hunting with my father and Uncle Russell. There were numerous coveys of quail on the Cobb place. Uncle Russell always kept a pen of bird dogs. I loved roving the fields on crisp fall days, watching the dogs hunt and point. I was a fairly good shot, and so were my father and Uncle Russ, so we usually had plenty of quail for the table.

Uncle Russ once gave me a puppy, a little white, long-haired setter. I named her Queenie. She was one of the few pet dogs I ever had, and I had her for several years until one day my father took her over to the Cobb place to teach her to hunt. She was a poor hunter, running up and flushing every covey they found, so Uncle Russ shot her and killed her. With a twelve-gauge shotgun. It was bird shot, but it was close range. I was pretty devastated but my father lectured me that a bird dog that wouldn't hunt was worthless.

I did a lot more fishing than hunting, from an early age on. My father and some other men had a fishing lake over in Greene

County, and we went over there a lot. And I fished in the rivers and the slews and tributaries. I loved roaming the swamps between the rivers in a skiff. I had a good friend, Nicky Braswell, who had played on the same team with me in Babe Ruth League (he was a catcher). He was a year ahead of me in school. I discovered, visiting his house, that he tied his own flies. He had a complete fly-tying outfit in his room. His father owned a hardware store downtown so Nicky had plenty of equipment. He let me borrow one of his fly rods.

Nicky knew an elderly gentleman named Nap Beasley. Nap was a colorful, grizzled old man of few words who did little else but fly-fish. He was fond of using his fly rod, with live bait, to catch grinnel, a bony, greasy bottom-feeding fish in the bar pits lining the highway leading to the river bridge north of town. Grinnel were not fit to eat, but they were large fish, most of them about two feet long and weighing three or four pounds, and they fought like tigers. They would bend a fly rod in half. They were a lot of fun to catch.

But Nap's specialty was fly-fishing for bream in farm ponds around the area. He came over to Nicky's house and we got out in the backyard and practiced casting. He taught me all the fine points of fly casting, and Nicky taught me how to tie flies. I ordered some equipment of my own, a tying vise, cork, feathers, rubber legs, and until I went off to college, I spent hours in my room working on my lures, cutting and painting popping bugs. Nap liked to use a little yellow popping bug over a bream bed, and the bream would tear it up.

One of the great pleasures of fly-fishing, which I enjoyed up until a few years ago, was that I could do it by myself. I liked being alone at a lake, the quiet stillness of the water, the silent peace that seemed to drift around me. It was a solitary happiness, a diversion from the chaos of living life, from the frenzied activities of day to day. I am never bored being alone, never lonely. I have been lonely in my life, but never from being alone.

There were other beer parlors than Red's Riverside Inn just across the Warrior River Bridge north of Demopolis, and there were state liquor stores over in Uniontown and in Boligee, both in wet counties and within easy driving distance. Boligee was little more than a crossroads hamlet with a liquor store; the store was there because Demopolis was. Though many of the small towns in the area, like Demopolis, were in dry counties, where it was not possible to buy liquor by the bottle (legally, anyway), the countryside and the outskirts were dotted with cafés and dance halls. They sold food—usually beef and chicken—and allowed you to bring in your bottle in a paper sack, put it under the table, and party to your heart's content. There was the Cotton Patch, over in Eutaw, a favorite of Bear Bryant's (he loved the fried chicken). There was the M&L Café in Demopolis and Green Gables in Uniontown, and a small place over near Greensboro that became one of our favorites, Over the Hill. Only young people, some in their early teens, went to Over the Hill.

What had been called "race music" in the forties was giving way to the new phenomenon, rock and roll. Lester Crawford and I loved it, and as soon as we got our driver's licenses, we rode around listening to Little Richard, Elvis, The Platters, Bo Didley, and Jerry Lee Lewis. There was a small, 250-watt radio station in Demopolis: WXAL, The Voice of the Black Belt. There was an announcer there, John Cooper, who did the *Mr. Boogie Man* show in the afternoons, with rhythm and blues. Though he was a white man, he announced with a heavy black accent. At night he played rock and roll.

The station was on Highway 80, and there was a circular driveway in the front. Lester and I started going out there and parking and listening to the songs, watching John Cooper through the window. Soon other teenagers started doing that, too, and every night there would be ten or so cars parked in front. We danced on the driveway and shouted requests to John Cooper. Kids from as far away as Linden and Greensboro (about the limits of WXAL's coverage area) started showing up, and it became quite a tradition.

Lester and I usually started the evening with a visit to a beer joint across the river called The Good Lady's. It had another, fancier name, but everybody called it The Good Lady's, except Lester, who called it The Good Lady's Malt Liquor Emporium. Sometimes we bought six packs and took them out and rode around. Lester acquired the nickname *Balboa* (where it came from, I don't know) and the other guys called me Captain Billy. We made up a song: "We're Captain Billy's Troopers / We're riders of the night / We're dirty sons of bitches / and we'd rather fuck than fight!" We were never carded; the good lady, a nice old woman who ran the place, told us to throw our beers in the trash if a police car pulled in off the highway. One never did. Sometimes we went to Red's Riverside Inn and sat in the back room and ate catfish and greasy cheeseburgers while we guzzled down twenty-five-cent beer and listened to the jukebox from the front room.

When I first started working at the Marengo Theater, I started smoking unfiltered Chesterfields, Pall Malls, and Lucky Strikes. Lester never smoked, but he was the only one of us who didn't. And later in high school, when most of us were athletes, we didn't stop smoking except sporadically. (For some reason, I still dream about smoking more than drinking, and I haven't smoked since 1989.) Everybody smoked; my mother and father, my aunts and uncles, my sister.

A hard night out was rip roaring around the Black Belt, radio blaring, smoking cigarettes and drinking beer, singing "Captain Billy's Troopers." Sheffield Truck and Tractor Company, sometime in the late forties, had acquired the dealership for Pontiac cars and International trucks. So by the time I got my license, my father had a sizable used car lot. He gave me a car, an old pale blue Plymouth that was on its last legs. Its floorboard was rusting out, it was dented and scratched, and it had retread tires. But it ran. Lester came into town in his father's pickup truck. Sometimes we went in the truck, but mostly we went in my car. After about a year, the car stopped running and my father pronounced it not worth repairing.

My father refused to buy me another car. He never said anything, but I suspected he'd gotten wind of our shenanigans. He seemed to be pulling further away from me. Something was wrong, and I didn't know what it was. I was feeling my way, discovering my own passions: literature, writing, old stories, history. It did not occur to me that I was growing more distant from him and that it might have troubled him. He didn't care about my passions any more than I cared about his business. It had been obvious to me from the start that I would never be happy with a career like he had, and that must have struck him as a judgment on his values. He just seemed to begin to withdraw himself from me. Along about this time he seemed to grow increasingly more depressed, to worry a lot about money, and it came out in hostility toward me. It was the old story: I didn't seem to be able to do anything to please him. He snapped at me all the time. It was as though he didn't care to be around me very much.

He had a neat little 1952 Chevrolet two-door coupe on the lot. The top was red and the chassis was black. It had standard shift on the steering column and was roomy. By today's standards, the backseat was huge. I told him I wanted to buy it, and he laughed. Then he said I could buy it by paying him $50 a month until I paid off the full $500 price tag. I agreed. It was pretty reckless, as I only made about $50 a month at the Marengo Theater. But I had to have a car. And it was early spring and Henry Webb had promised me some hours at the Grove Drive In when it opened for the summer. I also briefly took a job at Business Equipment Company, a business on Washington Street owned by one of my parents' good friends. I drove around all over Marengo County taking orders for office supplies. I was fired because I went into an office down in Linden and the man running the place said, laughing, when I walked in, "No, we don't want anything, get the hell out of here," so I said "Yes, sir," and left. Mr. Leet, the owner of

Business Equipment, complained that the man only wanted me to joke and talk with him before he placed his usual order. The man was annoying to me, and I wasn't about to jump through hoops for him. Mr. Leet suggested that perhaps I wasn't cut out to be a salesman, I agreed, and that part-time job was terminated.

Lester wasted no time in dubbing my car The Red and Black Bullet. I drove that car from then until I finished college and went off to Nashville to graduate school. It was a great car. Until toward the end, when something went wrong with the transmission and it wouldn't stay in gear. I would be driving down the road when suddenly the thing would pop up into neutral and the engine would roar like it was coming back there with me, while the car started coasting and slowing down. I could push it back into gear and continue on. I devised a solution myself. I bent a coat hanger and hooked it underneath the seat. After I put the car in high, I would hook the other end of the coat hanger around the gear shift lever. Whenever it threatened to pop out, it would grind against the coat hanger and I'd push it back down. My solution worked beautifully.

One night a bunch of us went to Over the Hill. We packed into The Red and Black Bullet. Lester was along, and Sally George, who was the younger sister of twin girls who were in my class. Sally was as cute as a three-week-old puppy. She had a saucy little figure and a ponytail that flapped in the breeze. And she was about my height. We loved to dance together, and went at it with a passion. And we were good. Doing the Bop! Come on Baby, Let the Good Times Roll! We went out together for a couple of years, on dance dates. We were not really "dating," not as boyfriend and girlfriend. Sally made it clear that she thought of me as a brother. The other people in the car were Angie Webb and a new friend of mine, Pat Brasfield, to whom I would grow quite close and who would eventually marry Jayne and become my brother-in-law. A big crowd from Demopolis was at Over the Hill that night, and we all sat around a long table. You could buy hard liquor at Over the Hill, and that night I bought a half gallon of Smirnoff Vodka.

All the way home we were drunk, singing "Waltz Me Around Again, Willie" at the tops of our voices. We sang the filthiest verses we could think of, beginning with "the boy from Nantucket." We sang, "There once was a man named McGroot / who had warts all over his root / they removed all of these / and now when he pees / McGroot holds his root like a flute. / Eye, yie yie yie / in China they never serve chili / so sing me another verse / that's worse than the other verse, / and waltz me around again, Willie!" We sang, "Roll me over in the clover and do it again!" We sang "Captain Billy's Troopers." We were young, and happy, and we didn't give a shit for anything. Sally was a real dirt road sport; she would later marry my cousin Mitch Cobb, and she has been a part of our family for many years. I see her all the time and e-mail with her. Angie had been my friend since we were children down on Commissioners Street, and she remains my friend. She was driving my car that night, the soberest one of us (not because she hadn't been drinking as much, but because Angie could drink everybody else under the table), and somewhere between Uniontown and Demopolis we picked up a hitchhiker, a young soldier who crowded himself into the backseat. As we progressed toward home, the soldier became increasingly more and more agitated at our drunkenness, at our loud singing, and when we came into town, he asked to be let out of the car. We wouldn't let him out. We drove around and around, singing and laughing, finally letting the shaken boy out on the corner in front of the hospital.

Lester and I would sometimes go inside WXAL and sit in the control room with John Cooper while he played the records. One night Lester suggested that the two of us go into the other control room and be "co-hosts" with John, which we did. Before long we were doing it regularly, and everybody loved it. Lester was so witty and funny that he soon had quite a following, and between the two of us we seemed to know every rock and roll song there was. Many years later, after I had published a couple of novels and was teaching at Montevallo, there came a late-night phone call. It was Lester, calling from a bar in Washington. He said he was having a debate with another fellow at the bar and they had put a bet on it, and he wanted me to take the phone and give the fellow the answer to one question. I agreed. "Who recorded 'In the Still of the Night'?" Lester asked. He gave the phone over to the other guy. "The Five Satins," I said, and I heard Lester yelling "Goddamit, I told you so! Ha ha ha ha!"

The owner of the radio station was a man named Mack Jordan, who was a good friend of my father's, so I knew him. John Cooper had told me there were some part-time hours opening up at the station, so I asked Mack Jordan for a job. He gave me one, and offered me considerably more an hour than I was making at the Marengo Theater and the Grove, though I continued to work there as well. I was still in high school and working two jobs, able to pay for my car and achieve a little independence. I no longer had to annoy my father by asking him for money all the time.

Both Mack Jordan and Henry Webb were willing to let me work flexible hours. Which was a good thing, because when I was a junior, I went out for football. I was five foot five inches tall and weighed one hundred fifty pounds. By the next year, when I was a senior and a starter on the team, I had grown one inch and put on five pounds. I went out for the backfield. I spent my junior season mostly sitting on the bench. I got to play a couple of times, but I hardly distinguished myself. Once, when we were beating Perry County High School about 60 to nothing, the coach sent the second and third teams in to mop up. We were on their five yard line, about to score again, when the quarterback gave me the ball over right tackle and I fumbled. Perry County recovered.

The coach at DHS was a man named E. D. "Chink" Lott. He was legendary, one of the finest coaches in the history of Alabama high school football. He had coached for many years at Anniston High School, a much larger school in the eastern part of the state, and the stadium there was named for him. He had puffy eyes and a sagging, vaguely Oriental-looking face, a heavyset man on short, stubby legs. He smoked a full bent pipe and reeked of Prince Albert tobacco and often of bourbon whiskey. The rumor was that Skipper, as we called him, had been fired at Anniston for drinking in front of his boys. He was a football genius. In 1951, his third team in Demopolis had gone undefeated, unscored on until the last game of the season, when they beat Linden 49 to 6. On Thanksgiving Day, they beat A. G. Parrish High in Selma, a school three times as big as DHS, 39 to 0 in Parrish's own stadium.

I adored Chink Lott, as did most of the other boys who played for him. He was profane, mean as hell, and drove us hard, but we knew that's what we were there for and that it would pay off. In fall camp my senior year, 1955, I was still in the backfield (we ran a tight T formation), but shortly before the season started, he switched me to guard. I worked hard. Skipper made me think I could play the game well, and so I did. He gave me the kind of confidence that Doc Knight had given me with baseball. I was a pulling guard on offense, a linebacker on defense. It was great fun. We won the Black Belt Conference title, and I made all-conference guard. (You can look it up!)

Lester wore a coat and tie on Friday nights for the games. I think he was the only one there dressed that way. He would sit up in the stands, and when the Coke vendor came by, he would pass the money down and yell, "Pour 'bout half that one out and pass it up to me!" Then he would fill it up from the bottle in his pocket. Once, in one of my rare shining moments, I intercepted a pass in the flats and ran it back down to the opposing team's end zone. One of their men upended me at the goal line, feet over head, and I turned a complete flip before crashing to the turf in the end zone. My head was woozy, and as I was shaking it to clear it, I saw and heard two things: Lester, in the stands, grinning from ear to ear. "You got your ass busted on that one, Cobb," he yelled. And a group of black people sitting in the end zone, where they had to sit when they came to our football games. "That's Mista Billy," I heard several of them yell. I had scored the only touchdown of my short career.

During my last two years of high school, I began to suffer from a terrible condition that persisted for several years. Some days I would break out in large red welts, all over my body, but especially my face. My face would be all distorted, my eyes swollen almost shut. It seemed to be more severe in those areas of my body where the skin was tight, like my scalp and the crack of my ass. It itched like crazy and was extremely uncomfortable. I went to our family doctor, who had no clue as to what was going on. My father's reaction was to scowl at me and say, "Billy, did you *job* today?" (*Job* was the Cobb euphemism for shit, and somehow from my father's mouth, *job* sounded far more vulgar than shit.) He seemed to be angry at me about it. Cobbs are not good nurses, impatient with illnesses of all kinds. I'm like that myself, as Loretta tells me often. Looking back, I think my father was frowning and angry because he was frustrated at not being able to do anything about it. It was out of his control. But what he conveyed to me was that he thought it was *my* fault that I had the hives.

I saw several doctors. None of them had any idea what the problem was. One of them suggested I see a doctor in Laurel, Mississippi, who was a specialist in hives. My mother and I drove down there in her Pontiac. The doctor examined me and poked me, did blood work. He decided it was nerves. He gave me a new drug called Valium. It seemed to help a little, but not very much. The hives would last a day or two and then disappear, only to pop out again in a couple of weeks. I had to keep a log of what I ate and drank, and any other medicines I took. The only thing consistent over several months was that on some days I would have a headache (read: hangover) and take aspirin and break out in the hives. The doctor finally told me I was allergic to aspirin, but that the main problem was a nervous one.

The attacks of hives continued off and on until after Loretta and

I had been married a few years. They lasted a period of twelve or thirteen years before they went away for good, but I suffered a great deal in the meantime. People would stare at me, and I hated it.

During those high school years I became close to Donald Porter, who had been in my class for a long time. Donald and I had known each other as children, but we were never good friends until high school. Donald was the oldest boy in a large family presided over by his mother, a beautiful Creole woman from New Orleans named Olga. His father, a wealthy business man in imports and exports, was never home. Their farm was a dairy farm, and Donald, from an early age, had had to get up early in the morning to help with the milking. He rode the bus to school, and often had cow shit on his pants. Olga was loud and flamboyant; my image of her from those days is seated at a grand piano in the parlor of their spacious white house wearing a long dress or gown with a glass of Scotch and soda perched on the piano. She drank a lot, and so did Donald. It was at the Porters' house that I learned to drink Scotch. Their brand, which his father bought by the case, was Old Smuggler. It was the first house I'd ever been in where they played classical music. One night Donald sat me down, gave me a glass of Scotch, and had me listen, for the first time, to Beethoven's Ninth Symphony, all the way through. And they had many books which had actually been read. The Porters lived an elegant lifestyle. One night when we were seniors, Olga had a bunch of us to dinner and, after a long cocktail hour, served a whole roast suckling pig with an apple in its mouth.

Pat Brasfield became one of my very best friends and later, of course, married Jayne. He was from an old and prominent family. It was his cousin Kirvin who had saved me from the devil pony. Pat's father, Samuel Patton Hand Brasfield, was dead; his mother had remarried while they were living down in Thomasville and they moved back to Demopolis. He was the great-great-grandson of Williamson Allen Glover, one of the founding patriarchs of

Demopolis and the builder of both Rosemount, an elegant, columned antebellum mansion across the river in Greene County, and Bluff Hall, which he built for his daughter Sara Serena and her husband, Francis Strother Lyon.

Our English teacher at DHS was an accomplished and dedicated woman named Wynelle Gantt. She was brilliant. (She was very attractive, too, a fact not lost on horny post-adolescents.) She taught English literature to an entire generation, from *The Canterbury Tales* through Shakespeare to the Victorians. She had us write term papers and essays. Donald Porter and I discovered that we both wanted to be writers, and we would get together and talk about it. We were both avid readers. I still read every book my mother brought home from her "study club," book club stuff like *Forever Amber*, *The Last Time I Saw Paris*, and the historical novels of James Street. My mother joined the Book of the Month Club. I read every one that came to the house. With me, the reading was a secret; I didn't want my other friends to know I did it, since it was not exactly the masculine pursuit that a budding young "good ol' boy" should aspire to. I was still losing myself in imaginary worlds, a practice that has persisted down to the present day.

Reading is not now, and never was, just a pastime with me, an escape from life; rather it is an escape more deeply *into* life. Reading makes me more fully alive, allows me to live more than one life, and I knew even back then it was incalculably most important for that reason. I knew that instinctively, and Donald and Pat knew it as well. That we felt that way made us different, separated us in some fundamental ways from the culture we were growing up in.

I vividly remember when Mrs. Gantt assigned *Silas Marner*. I was shocked that a book that was actually assigned in school could be so good. I devoured it. Donald liked it, too, and we were soon discussing books and literature after class with Mrs. Gantt. We admitted to her that we wanted to write fiction. She did not laugh at us; she encouraged us. She was the mentor that guided us through those years.

Mrs. Gantt told us that there was another boy in the school who wanted to be a writer. We both knew Pat Brasfield, though not well. He was younger than us, in Jayne's class. Pat had already acquired a reputation as a wild man. He drank hard and drove fast. He got into fights on the school campus. He was tall and blond and wore his hair long like James Dean. He idolized James Dean, as most of us did, but Pat actually looked like him. Soon Pat was joining me and Donald on our forays over to The Good Lady's and to long Scotch-soaked bull sessions out at Donald's house. We argued about books. Don insisted that *By Love Possessed* by James Gould Cozzins was a great novel. I disagreed. We discovered Kerouac and John O'Hara. We decided that Michener was a fraud. We all loved *The Catcher in the Rye*, but Pat was especially crazy about it. He identified with Holden Caulfield so much that he even started calling his little sister Nancy "Phoebe."

The three of us would drive over to Tuscaloosa to go to the bookstores. In spite of its degree of sophistication, Demopolis had no bookstore, and it still doesn't, even though so many of its native sons were and are literary persons. I bought my first copy of *Ulysses* in Tuscaloosa, and the collected stories of Carson McCullers. I picked up a new first edition of *On the Road*, which I still have. Pat also identified with Neal Cassidy. After Donald and I had gone off to college, Pat ran away and hitchhiked to Mexico with a friend.

On several occasions, we bought several six-packs of beer and drove over to Rosemount, Pat's ancestral home. Nobody lived there. It was mostly a big, deserted shell, but we discovered that there was still lots of old furniture remaining upstairs. We jimmied a window and, with flashlights, went up to the second floor, where we propped up in a big old musty four-poster bed and drank our beer and imagined that we were living during Williamson Allen Glover's time, with the slaves and cotton fields and the Civil War. We would describe to each other what the people were like. Pat had an old tinted photograph of a painting of Serena Glover that had belonged to his father, and we were all in love with her.

The torrents of our creativity would surge. In our minds we wrote exciting and romantic novels of that old, dead time, which remained very much alive in our imaginations.

The place has since been restored. When I was a little boy—before it fell into ruin—my father used to take me over there to fish in the lake in front of the house. The family that lived there then, the Legares, were descendants of the Glovers. It was right out of William Faulkner, except that it was real. I would see old Mrs. Legare walking in the yard, in the shadow of that huge old white house going faded gray, long, unruly salt-and-pepper hair, flowing dark dress, as spooky as a ghost. She had a son, Bud Legare, who was severely deformed and in a wheelchair. One of the black men on the place used to bring Bud in to the movies at the Marengo Theater, and he scared little children with his grotesque spasms and squirming in the wheelchair. An interesting footnote: The name was pronounced "Legree," and Harriet Beecher Stowe got the name *Simon Legree* when she once met a member of the family. How could the three of us *not* turn into writers?

I soon learned just how outrageous Pat could be. There was a man over in Montgomery, Star Smith, who taught a course in creative writing. Mrs. Gantt had told him about us. He asked her if we wanted to come over there and read some of our fiction to his class. Donald and I both refused, pleading that we didn't have anything that was good enough to read to anybody, but Pat said he'd like to. He invited me to come along with him.

We drove over to Montgomery. The class was obviously a continuing education class of some sort, with mostly middle-aged or older people. Star Smith was a pompous man who immediately began trying to impress me and Pat with how much he knew about fiction writing, about Southern fiction in general. We all sat around a big table. There was much "clever" repartee, and Pat kept cutting his eyes at me, a sly smile on his face. When it came his time, be began to read his story. He had told me it was a new story and he was going to surprise me with it. He was going to blow them away. As he began reading, the story sounded familiar; two paragraphs in I realized that he was reading, in a calm, controlled voice, Carson McCullers's masterful, and *famous*, story "A Tree, a Rock, a Cloud." I was astonished. Surely, I thought, some of these people, who, after all, are writing stories and presumably read them, have read it before. The people around the table, including Star Smith, listened with rapt, respectful attention, as well they should have. When Pat finished, he accepted all their praise and plaudits graciously and humbly. Star Smith was impressed out of his mind. He kept saying to Pat, "You ought to write a novel, you ought to write a novel." We laughed all the way back to Demopolis.

It was a tradition in Demopolis that the senior trip was a week in Washington and New York. Each class worked for years, holding car washes, selling candy, organizing bake sales and raffles, to raise the money to go. It was probably the biggest deal of high school. Our class left on the train, the old Southern Crescent that ran between New Orleans and Washington/New York. We stayed up all night on the train, playing poker and sipping contraband liquor we'd sneaked aboard. The boys lusted after the girls, and lots of couples managed to "make out" during the trip. We went first to Washington and checked into the Mayflower Hotel. We did all the sights and monuments and had a great time. Then we reboarded the train for New York. We stayed at the old Taft Hotel in Midtown. We ate at Sardi's, went to see *The Pajama Game* with John Rait and Shirley McClaine, went to Radio City Music Hall. Several of us boys found a strip club. You could watch the girls dance as long as you wanted to so long as you ordered a drink. They were beautiful, sexy girls. I remember the bartenders getting amused that so many of us ordered Tom Collinses. The only strippers I'd seen before were two young girls at a carnival in town. I'd gone out there one night after work. There was a tent show called "The Streets of Paris." Men and boys were standing around behind a barrier made from sawhorses with a tarp thrown over them. Music started and the two girls, hardly more than children, came out and simply shucked off their clothes and jumped around. The next day I was startled to look up and see the two of them coming into the Marengo Theater to go to a matinee, both of them looking like all the other teenaged girls there. To see them that way, in their blouses and pedal pushers, made me feel incredibly melancholy.

Donald, Lester, and I walked the streets a lot, just getting the feel of New York. We loved it and dreamed of the day we'd live there ourselves. Donald and I remembered those walks years later, when he was living in Manhattan. When one of my plays was in rehearsal, during the days Donald and I would go for long walks and eat breakfast or lunch together. The most vivid memory of that initial trip to New York that has stuck with me all these years was the taste of my first martini. Don and I sat at the bar in a place near Times Square. With the first sip I knew I'd never tasted anything so sublime in my entire life. I had found the true nectar of heaven.

Seven

My father told me grimly that he could not afford to send me to college. Donald was going off to Sewanee to major in English. Lester was going to Auburn to enroll in the preveterinary medicine program. I wanted to go to Birmingham-Southern College, where Winston was enrolled, but it is an expensive, private liberal arts college. I applied for scholarships, but I had not studied much in high school, settling for B's in everything but English courses, so I could get no scholarship help. My second choice would have been the University of Alabama in Tuscaloosa. One night my father was waiting up for me when I came in from work. He told me he had found a way for me to go to school. He had talked to a friend, Mr. Jack Kinzer, who went to the Presbyterian Church. Mr. Kinzer was district manager with Alabama Power Company, and I could join their co-op program and go to Auburn to study electrical engineering. I told my father that I did not want to go to Auburn, and I definitely did not want to study electrical engineering. He said he had found this for me, so I had a choice. I could take it and go to college or I could join the Army. He didn't care which I did. But he was not paying to send me to college.

I have often pondered, in later years, how my life might have turned out if I'd joined the Army. Maybe the regimentation, the discipline, would have been good for me; I would have been forced to be a part of a community of men that I might not otherwise have chosen to pal around with. Maybe I would have forged friendships that lasted. It would certainly have shaped me differently, making me conform to a group and its principles and rules, which might have toned down my lifelong distrust of authority. On the other hand, it might have encouraged my rebellious nature. And I could have been one of those first Americans killed in Vietnam, in 1959.

I finally agreed to join the Alabama Power Company program. After all, Lester was going to Auburn and he was delighted that I'd be there, too. He suggested we room together in the dorm when I finally came, during the winter quarter. At least I would be in college.

It was difficult for me to deal with what I perceived as hostility toward me on the part of my father. Coupled with my chronic plague of hives, his apparent lack of confidence and belief in me was deeply troubling and reaffirmed all my feelings of inferiority. From the perspective of years of therapy, I now think my father had not counted on having a son who had no interest at all in his business, the career he had devoted his life to. But I had none, and I didn't try to soften my distaste. I couldn't bear the thought of working at Sheffield's, selling cars. Selling *anything*. He found himself with a son who wanted to be a *writer*, for God's sake, who didn't like to hunt and preferred to go fishing by himself. My life must have seemed as foreign to him as his did to me.

We were never close. I don't think we ever had a serious conversation about anything until quite late in our lives, and then only out of necessity. He had no patience for talk. I never knew, for example, what he really believed where religion was concerned. He never once, in all my young life, asked me what I wanted to do with myself as an adult. He joked about it. In his cups he would say to other people, "Billy's gonna be a rich doctor, so he can take care of me in my old age," and then laugh. Had he been able to see ahead about fifty years into the future, he wouldn't have found it so funny.

He never expressed a hint of sympathy or regret that I couldn't go to the colleges I desired, and of course I read that as his not giving a damn. I'm still not absolutely sure that was not the case. Everybody loved Sledge Cobb. He was "good as gold," people would say. Nobody who knew him casually would ever believe he could be as cold and uncaring as he was toward me, nobody except my cousins Mitch and Linda Cobb, who had to deal with their father, Aubrey, who was my father's first cousin and lifelong good friend. From what Mitch has told me, Aubrey was far worse than Sledge.

Where was my mother in all this, I can hear you asking. Good question. She nurtured me, and I loved her deeply until the day she died. She was a beautiful woman, and smart, much smarter in many ways than my father, and creative. I found an essay that she had written in college, tucked away in an old trunk in the attic, entitled "The Storm," about a small tornado that swept through Livingston and blew the second story off the administration building. I complimented her on it and she seemed embarrassed. She chided me for poking around in places that were none of my business. My father read the newspapers every day, but my mother didn't. She had no interest in current events, in what was going on in the rest of the world. She read magazines: *Ladies' Home Journal*, *The Saturday Evening Post*, and *Good Housekeeping*. She read the novels from her book and study clubs, and played bridge. There was rarely much music in our house; after the early fifties there was usually the background noise of the television set playing.

My mother would not have thought of intervening between my father and me. I think people of my parents' generation, having come of age during the Great Depression and World War II, having been raised by parents who had not shaken off the strictures of Victorianism and Puritanism, had rigid, firmly set ideas of the roles of parents, of men and women. Mothers had certain responsibilities toward their children, fathers had others, and they were separate and clearly defined. It was not my mother's duty to interfere with her husband's raising of their son. This seems unbelievably quaint to me today and hard to accept about reasonably intelligent people who lived through most of the twentieth century, but I believe it was true in the case of my parents. Donald's mother, Olga, did *all* the parenting in their family and ran the farm as well, driving around in her Cadillac in muddy rubber boots. She was the object of some provincial curiosity and gossip among other women in the town.

When September came, Lester went off to Auburn, Donald to Sewanee (he carried a case of Old Smuggler to keep in his dorm room), and Pat went back to high school. I went to work in the local office of Alabama Power Company. It was a district office, with Mr. Kinzer the supervisor, two engineers, and several secretaries and clerks. I worked in a long back room with drafting boards, maps, the engineers' desks, and my desk, a dull gray metal one exactly like the others. I found myself doing what I had feared most: working in an office. Shuffling papers. The engineers were an odd tandem of guys. They both wore "uniforms," khaki pants and shirts with APCo over the pockets. One, a man named David, was an almost total slob; his clothes were wrinkled and his belly hung out over his belt. The other's clothing was ironed and crisp, there was not a hair out of place on his head, and he moved and did everything with a kind of prissy precision. He lined up his cigarette pack precisely with his ashtray on his desk, which was neat and uncluttered. His name was Mr. Brown.

The saving grace of the situation was that I got to go out in the field with one of the engineers two or three times a week. When a new power line was going up, or there was new service going to a farmhouse, we would go and measure off the spans and draw up a map, driving stakes where the poles were to be set. The line crew would come along later and string the lines according to our designs, and once they were finished, I would update the maps in the office. I enjoyed getting out in the fine fall weather, especially when I went with David. We would take our time, poke around, smoke cigarettes, and take three-hour lunches in various country cafés. When I went with Mr. Brown, it was all business. Except when *he* wanted to pull off a joke: Once he sent me into a pasture where there was a yearling bull with six-inch horns and I had to scramble over a fence to keep from being gored. Mr. Brown thought that was funny as hell. He was always prodding me to tell him that David slacked off and didn't work very hard, but I wouldn't. Both of them were pretty lackluster, but I liked David okay.

The work could be grueling, but exciting at times. Once we had to use machetes to cut through the thick undergrowth of a swamp for about a hundred yards. We killed three water moccasins that day. And once during the fall there was a violent storm. Lines went down, and I was called out along with all the other employees in the area and found myself on the roof of a motel out on the highway, where a TV antenna had fallen on a power line. I used a long pole with a hook on it to trip a circuit breaker on a transformer while the wind buffeted me and the rain lashed me.

And that autumn I became a sportscaster. WXAL broadcast Demopolis High School football games and I partnered with Austin Caldwell, the manager of the station, in doing play-by-play. I continued to work at the station on weekends and some nights a week. Mack Jordan seemed to like me. He told me that when I came back home in the spring, he would have some hours for me.

After Christmas, I headed over to Auburn to start my freshman year during the winter quarter. I got off to a terrible start. In all the excitement of leaving, I broke out in the hives and arrived on campus an anxious and nervous freshman, with my face reddened and distorted. Lester and I moved into a small room in Magnolia Hall Dormitory, near the football stadium. I was pleased to be with him, but I didn't really want to be there. I felt uncomfortable, very much out of place. It was a kind of chronic, lasting anxiety attack. Every walk across campus, every new class, was a trial.

Lester knew a lot of people, and people seemed to know him. Unlike me, he made friends easily wherever he went. He is probably the most likable person I've ever known. He had friends all over Magnolia Hall, all over the Auburn campus. He used to joke that one day he would run for governor of Alabama and I would be his speech writer. He was being rushed by a small fraternity, Sigma Pi. I had been invited over to Tuscaloosa to some Kappa Alpha parties while I was still in high school, and while I enjoyed the drinking and carousing and pretty girls, something about the forced camaraderie made me uneasy. I had the sense that the Demopolis boys who'd invited me had done so only out of obligation toward a hometown boy who wanted to come there to school. I hadn't really thought I'd have much to do with fraternities, but I went along to Sigma Pi with Lester. The boys there seemed to like me and began to rush me. There was a lot of getting me off by myself to talk somberly to me about "loyalty for life" while they were knocking down beers. I struggled to keep a straight face. I could see that they all took it very seriously.

Since I was a freshman, I had to wear a little blue and orange beanie with an A on it. There were supposed to be dire consequences if you were ever caught without it on. Apparently by winter quarter most people had lost interest in the tradition, so I threw mine away and nobody seemed to notice. I took history, freshman English, chemistry, and remedial noncredit algebra. I made C's in all of them but remedial algebra, which I failed. I was excused from PE because of my heart murmur, but I had to take ROTC. Auburn was a Land Grant Institution, and all the men had to enroll in ROTC, and I detested it. On drill days I had to wear my uniform to class because I didn't have time to go back to the dorm to change, and if you were late, you got demerits that you had to work off with extra duty. The uniform was ill fitting, stiff, and scratchy, and I felt like a total fool wearing it to class.

We had to wear all the brass and keep it polished and shine the shoes until they glinted. One day a week, right after lunch, we had to march on the parade ground over near the armory, carrying heavy M1 rifles left over from World War II. If you made a misstep, you got a demerit. (I never got the hang of "Right oblique, march!") We had military classes taught by uptight, all-American types, who looked natural in *their* uniforms. We studied battle tactics and learned to break down, clean, and restore the rifles. I have no idea how many demerits I accumulated, but I know it was a bunch. Before I later withdrew, I just quit going to ROTC. I made an F, and as far as I know, the demerits are still on the books over there, because I never worked them off.

I had never studied much in high school. I discovered that I needed to learn how to do it. Lester was very studious; I guess he had been all along. Boys that age don't swap stories about how much they study. Or at least we didn't. Lester had been in the Beta Club with me, and he had the third highest average in our class, after Alan Koch and Jerre Levy. I got dismissed from the Beta Club when I made a C in algebra; my mother swore I did it on purpose. Now I was astonished to see how much my old friend studied. He took all his classes seriously. I didn't know anybody who was like that. Donald, Pat, and I took novels seriously, but in my mind that was different. Lester, for casual reading between his schoolwork assignments, was reading the goddam *encyclopedia*, A to Z, cover to cover! I realized how far I had to go, how very little intellectual curiosity I had.

The fact that I never passed anything—test, homework assignments, anything—in my remedial algebra course confirmed my sincere belief that I was not cut out to be an electrical engineer. I enjoyed the chemistry and did pretty well in it. I liked my history course because I liked the professor. He was a weird bird named

D. Roy Sharpe. There was a member of the varsity basketball team named Jimmy Fibbe in the class, and Mr. Sharp told us the first day that Jimmy Fibbe was the only one who could count on making an A. Once, when my car was in the shop, I was hitch-hiking back to Auburn on a Sunday afternoon. It started to storm when I was just east of Selma. A motorcycle stopped. It was D. Roy Sharpe. I hopped on the back and he rode me all the way to Auburn in the rain. I was put into the advanced freshman English class, taught by an earnest young man who was probably a graduate student. I clearly remember reading *The Mayor of Casterbridge* and *Tess of the D'Urbervilles.*

I went to lots of parties at fraternity houses and often got drunk. After I had a few drinks, I would dance and flirt with the girls. I quickly acquired a reputation as a hell-raiser, and I did nothing to disappoint anyone who had that opinion. I got long, literary letters from Donald. Some he typed. When he wrote them by hand, I could barely read them. I didn't know if his handwriting was really that strange or if it was an affectation. He seemed to be taking courses worthy of Oxford or the Sorbonne.

He was writing a novel, and so was Pat. (I never saw a page of either one of them.) I wasn't writing anything at all. I felt out of sync with everything and everybody. I was a weirdo, like D. Roy Sharpe. Everyone else seemed to have found their own comfortable niches and were thriving. During the days I suffered from a lot of anxiety, but at night I had a few drinks and came alive. The first few sips would be sweet, soothing, and medicinal. A balm. Whiskey was truly an antidote for me: When I had the hives, a couple of drinks would make them go away.

At the end of the quarter I went home to my parents' house and moved back into my old room for my season of work with the power company. It was the same old drudgery, the same tired old jokes, the smell of Mr. Brown's cigarettes. (He was the only one Mr. Kinzer let smoke in the office; why that was, I have no idea.) When the bream were on the beds, me and The Red and Black

Bullet would go over to the lake in the late afternoons with our little yellow popping bugs and my trusty six-pack of Pabst. Sometimes Pat went with me, and we often visited The Good Lady's and spent countless late nights drinking coffee and bullshitting at the Cherokee Café out on Highway 80. The most exciting thing that happened all spring was when the president of the Southern Company, the parent company of APCo, came to visit at the office. Everyone was beside themselves. You were supposed to treat him like the Pope. I thought he was a swaggering jerk.

Pat asked Jayne to be his date for the prom. The night of the dance he showed up at the door in a tux and high-top white tennis shoes. My mother almost fainted. She was furious that Pat had "ruined" her daughter's junior prom, but Jayne took it in stride. My mother got over the tennis shoes. She needed to, because Jayne and Pat eventually married and produced my mother's first three grandchildren. Sad to say, she never got over until the day she died the heartbreak of their difficult marriage and divorce.

When summer came, I went back to school. Lester was in Gallion for the summer, and I lived in Magnolia Hall by myself. Since there were so many fewer students in the summer session, I requested a private room and got it. Donald was home from Sewanee, Pat was out of school, and I burned up the highway going back and forth from Auburn in the Bullet. I would spend long weekends in Demopolis, when we frequented The Good Lady's, took six-packs to the Drive-In Theater, and sat around at Donald's house all night listening to music and drinking Scotch, talking about books and writing. We did a lot of water-skiing on Lake Demopolis, and once I made an extended trip to Panama City, Florida, with several other boys. We went to a place called "The Hangout," an open air place on the beach where kids went to dance. I was too sheepish to ask a girl to dance. I suffered a kind of anxiety attack and broke out in the hives. We had checked into a rundown motel way off the beach, and I had to stay in the room. I recall, with some amusement now, that the other boys decided they were going to find a prostitute. I was actually relieved I didn't have to go. They went into the bathroom one by one and masturbated in a passionless, businesslike way so they could last longer and get their money's worth.

I had so lost interest in anything scholarly I was supposed to be doing in school that I honestly can't remember what courses I took during that summer quarter. My intellectual curiosity was near zero. I had no direction at all, and I didn't even know I'd lost it. Oddly, this experience equipped me as well as the graduate courses I took for my future college teaching career, as I later taught many sections of freshman English; I was an advisor to numerous confused, disoriented students who felt invisible, irretrievable, and I could be empathic as well as sympathetic.

I spent a lot of time alone, reading in my room, walking the streets. I had finally faced up to the fact that I couldn't continue this way, and I determined that I would quit the co-op program and drop out of Auburn. I didn't know what the hell I was going to do, but I knew I had to go in another direction. I really didn't know enough of the world to be terribly frightened by it; I was still the provincial Southern boy. That I didn't know what I wanted to do—other than that ever-nagging desire to be a writer—or where I wanted to go seemed a source of strength to me.

My father hit the ceiling. He thought it was the most irresponsible thing I had ever done. I broke out in one of the worst cases of hives I'd had. I packed my car with my clothes, some of my books, my typewriter. I had saved a little money from my job at the power company. I decided that I would just drive away. I wanted to go to a city, so I chose Nashville. I said good-bye to everybody and drove north.

Eight

I had never lived in a city before, and I knew not a soul in Nashville. I just knew about Elvis recording there, and I had always been an admirer of country music. When I was a little boy visiting my grandparents in Gilbertown, we had always listened to the Grand Ole Opry on an old upright Philco radio in the parlor. We listened to Minnie Pearl and Roy Acuff, The Carter Family, Lester Flatt and Earl Scruggs. "From Ryman Auditorium, in Nashville, Tennessee, *The Grand Ole Opry!*" the announcer would shout. I suppose I had some vague, half-assed idea that I would somehow get into the country music business. Certainly not as a singer, but as an announcer or something. Maybe even the guy who yelled, "From Ryman . . . etc." I had no real plans other than I was going to write a novel, and I had not a clue as to how I would support myself. None of that seemed to matter, since I had left Auburn and electrical engineering behind. I knew even then that I had put one of the worst experiences of my life behind me.

Looking back from the perspective of my years, I see now that that was the beginning of my recovery. I had broken out of some of the constraints of my culture. At the same time, I had given up some of the basic values that I had relied on. I felt there was true value in being honest with myself, but I felt isolated, reclusive. It would take me many years to realize that—in my life at least—happiness as others defined it was an illusion.

I found a cheap room in a rooming house on Church Street, out near the Vanderbilt Campus just off West End Avenue. I could park the Bullet in the alley behind the house. My fellow tenants were a nighttime cab driver, a construction worker, and two elderly derelicts who shared a room and never went out. The place was run by a woman named Irene Rogers. She asked for two weeks in advance (I think the fee was $5 a week, but my memory may be faulty on that), told me I could keep Cokes in the refrigerator on the ground floor (my room was on the second floor, on a corner overlooking Church Street) and that I could not bring women in after dark. She stated that she "didn't take any shit." She asked me if I drank, and when I said, "Yes, ma'am," she chuckled and said, "It's a good man's failin'."

The recording industry was becoming increasingly more important in Nashville. It was not only Music City, U.S.A., as it called itself, but it was the place that dreams of music stardom went to die. (Both the construction worker and the cab driver told me they wrote songs; during the entire eight months I lived there, neither ever offered to sing me one. And I didn't request that they do so.) There were bars and clubs all over the city, with bands and singers. Down on Broad Street, below Ryman Auditorium, there was a row of pawn shops with their windows filled with guitars and cowboy boots that must have been hocked by disappointed people to buy a ticket home.

I had no notion of entering that world except in the most peripheral way. Interspersed with the recording studios were "schools" that taught music performance. In my exploring the city I saw a couple that were schools for radio announcers. One had a sign out front that said, BE A DISK JOCKEY. Even though I already *was* a disk jockey, I read their promotional material. They *guaranteed* that if you finished their course, they would find you a job as a radio announcer. They were closed, but I filled out a card with the phone number of the rooming house and put it through a slot on the door.

The cab driver slept all day, so the house was quiet. I heard rarely a peep out of the old derelicts. I would sometimes see them coming along the sidewalk with bottles of cheap wine in paper sacks. I wrote. I sat in my room, and on that old manual Underwood typewriter, I banged away at a novel about old Joe Bynymo in Demopolis. I abandoned it and began one about a young girl in Nashville. I had not the foggiest notion where I was going, but I managed to accumulate quite a few pages.

One day a call came and Mrs. Rogers yelled up the stairs for me. It was the announcers' school. They had reviewed my application, they said, and asked me to come in. The two men who interviewed me wore loud plaid sport jackets and cowboy boots. One was old and one was young. They had a faux control room for practice, with racks of record albums. I had not been in there five minutes before I realized that it was not for me. For one thing, the tuition was exorbitant, something I could never have afforded, though I didn't have to pay it all at once. They had a scholarship plan whereby I could pay my fees monthly after I had a job. The men were so slick they were slimy, and I did not like them. I told them I would think about it. I didn't. I went back to my room and vowed that I would one day write a novel about a naive young person coming to the big city. (I had actually already begun it. See *Coming of Age at the Y* some years later.)

My money was running low and I knew that sooner or later I was going to have to find a job. Mrs. Rogers put *The Nashville Tennessean* in the parlor every morning, and one day I found an ad for a job at Krystal Hamburgers. The job was working the graveyard shift, 11 p.m. till 7 a.m. at a little 24-hour Krystal on 21st Street. I would still be able to write some during the day and early evening, and I figured I'd be able to eat there cheap. Since I'd been in Nashville, I'd eaten at the Krystal a lot. I liked the cheeseburgers, chili, and breakfasts, and they were inexpensive. I went to the diner and talked with the manager. The diner was across Hillsborough Road from Peabody College and just down the road from Vanderbilt. I got the job and I worked there until I left Nashville.

I liked working at the Krystal. Like the colored balcony at the Marengo Theater, it was one of the best jobs I ever had. The other two boys who worked the night shift were about my age, and in the months I worked there, a steady stream of boys and young men about the same age came to work there and quit. We had to wear white shirts, white aprons, and little white paper hats. When I started, I was lowest in seniority, so I had to be the one to pull the heavy wooden grates from behind the counter, haul them out into the back alley, and hose off the grease and mashed bits of buns. Then I had to mop the floor and replace the grates. This was always done during the wee hours of the morning because it was the slowest time. Because of the turnover, it wasn't long before I had moved up and no longer had to do that chore.

The graveyard shift was the slowest one of the day anyway. Things didn't really pick up until about five thirty, when people started coming in for breakfast. You had to always keep hamburgers cooking on the grill, but there was never a rush. There was plenty of time to drink coffee and talk to the people who came in. Students, of course, from both Peabody and Vanderbilt, were there all hours of the night. And street people came in to warm their hands around a cup of coffee and slurp chili. Two women came in often, usually around two or three in the morning, and I figured they were prostitutes. They would eat bacon and eggs. They kidded me, told me I was "adorable." I'd never seen a prostitute before and I was certainly titillated. They were older than me, and I didn't think I could have afforded them.

I did have one girlfriend during my first time in Nashville, a student at Peabody. She was one of the most bizarre girls I'd met up until then. Aurora wore long gypsy skirts and T shirts with lots of beads. She had very large breasts and she didn't wear a bra, something I'd never seen before either. You could plainly see her large round nipples through the cloth. One of the boys who worked there would say, when she came in from outside, "Hey, headlights on high beam!" We struck up a friendship.

Aurora liked to read. We talked about novels we'd read. She was taking a course in the modern novel, and one of the things she said to me was "Hemingway is a macho jerk-shit." I didn't know what she was talking about half the time, but I tried to listen. She was taking the kind of courses I wanted to take. She was like some kind of informal college course in the novel that I needed. She let me read the books she bought for the course; I read *A Farewell to Arms* for the first time, and Joyce's *Portrait of the Artist as a Young Man.*

She lived off campus, and one morning she invited me to her place. She lived in a residential area south of Peabody, just off Franklin Pike, and we walked there. I was fairly surprised to learn that she lived in a garage in an alley behind a house. Not a converted garage, just a garage. With a dirt floor. There was an old iron bed, a sink, a portable toilet, and a hot plate. She told me she went over to North Hall, on the Peabody campus, to shower. I never knew what she was going to say next. She would jump from books to food to movies to music and back to books in one paragraph, unable to concentrate on any one thing very long.

The two of us spent a lot of time walking in Centennial Park. I would swipe buns from the Krystal and we'd feed the ducks at the lake. Aurora envied me my neat room when I finally asked her over there one night before I had to go to work. We had been shooting pool at a bar on West End when she said, "Let's go to your place. I want to see it." I had been hesitant. When I told her about Mrs. Rogers's rule about no girls allowed, she said, "She can go fuck herself." I have no idea what Aurora paid to rent the garage nor where she got her money from. She was a free spirit who never thought about tomorrow.

Donald and I exchanged letters regularly. Pat wrote me a couple of times. He and Jayne were still dating some, but they were not serious, he said. I got short, chatty letters from my mother. Never a word from my father. I did not drink very much during those months. I kept a bottle of bourbon in my room, but I rationed it. I didn't consciously think of myself as "on the wagon," since I never thought of myself as having a drinking problem.

Nine

After almost a year in Nashville, I was growing restless. I had already decided that I needed to move on, to move ahead, and I'd determined that I needed to get back in school. My friendship with Aurora lasted only a couple of months, and I didn't really make any other friends. I didn't have very much in common with the other boys who worked at the Krystal; most of them were devout Church of Christ who often tried to save my soul. I found that extremely annoying. I had thrown off Christianity, gotten it out of my life.

I was not a believer, and I can't say with any honesty that I ever have been, though Loretta and I would later both be confirmed in the Episcopal Church. We raised Meredith in the church, and for many years I was quite active, even serving on some diocesan committees and serving St. Andrew's in Montevallo as Senior Warden. I loved the aesthetics of the church, the ritual, the order. To me, the most appealing and satisfying aspect of the church was its Calendar, which seemed to me a paradigm for a good and orderly life, something against which I could see a relief of myself, a way of dealing with meaning and mortality. But the "sin and salvation" element of religion left me cold. I was troubled by the Virgin Birth, by the divinity of Christ, by the Resurrection, by the miracles that required, for me, pure blind faith. I questioned everything, and that wasn't good in the kind of Bible Belt culture in which I was raised. My parents thought I was obstinate, trying to get attention. I was told to shut up, to keep it to myself.

I've always felt that Christ's significance lay in his *humanity*, not in his divinity. Christ did not teach us how to die; he taught us how to live. So the transcendence of belief always eluded me. Even as a child I felt silly praying. In the Episcopal Church the prayers and the creeds were not emotional appeals but were a part of a ritual unchanged for centuries. To me, they were for the people reciting them, not messages to some elusive, supreme power beyond our comprehension. That I believed that way gave me a reassurance that I was part of some tradition, something larger than myself, and that was comforting to me, because the exact same words had been recited for almost two thousand years. During the quarter century I was an active Christian, I was often challenged for my beliefs by other people within the church, particularly priests that I'd meet; I was told that my refusal to believe in something like the Virgin Birth or the Resurrection was the supreme heresy, that the idea I could decide something like that for myself was blasphemous. If I didn't believe it, how could it be blasphemy? I was told that I was not a Christian, but a secular humanist; Jesus was not just a great moral teacher but God, a part of the Trinity. That was, and is, a difficult concept for me to grasp, just as the logic of the conceit that Jesus died to atone for our sins has always remained an elusive idea for me. The only way it makes any sense, for me, is to read it as entirely symbolic.

I formed all these beliefs under the influence of a Father Jack Bush, who reassured me that the Episcopal Church was the only one where you might be kneeling at the altar rail with a devout believer on one side of you and an agnostic on the other. I found that immensely appealing. Jack Bush was a charismatic priest who was the first full-time priest that St. Andrew's in Montevallo had ever had. Many of our friends were Episcopalians, especially Jeannie Robison and John Finlay, both of whom were teaching in the English Department at the college. We met Jack Bush at several parties around town. He drank heavily. He was the most intellectual "church person" I'd ever met. We started going to church occasionally, hung over or not; we were told that most of the people there were hung over, even the priest. His sermons were remarkable: none of that Bible thumping and judgmental moralizing I'd heard every Sunday of my youth. Jack Bush did not live by rules; morality for him was love for your fellow man. His Christianity was centered around this passage in the Eucharist, from the teachings of Christ: "You shall love the Lord your God with all your heart and soul and mind, and love your neighbor as yourself. *On these two commandments hang all the laws of the prophets.*" I emphasize the last sentence, because he felt strongly that if a Christian followed Christ's two commandments, then everything else in the New Testament—and the holdovers from the Old, like the Ten Commandments—was unnecessary, even irrelevant. He did not blink an eye when I told him of my disbelief in the miracles of the church. He told me they were symbolic and did not have to be taken literally. When I told him I didn't "love God," that I wasn't even sure there was a God, he said that God *was* perfection and love; it was in the *striving* toward love, in the living of that love, that we could find satisfaction and peace. It was totally unlike anything I'd heard in that stern gray stone church in Demopolis. Many years later, when I gave the eulogy for my brother-in-law Pat Brasfield in that church, an elderly lady of long acquaintance came up to me and said, "Billy, that is the most *Episcopal* sermon that was ever preached in this church!"

Jack Bush was a nonconformist, extremely controversial. Loretta and I became regular attendees, delighting in his outrageousness, though there were many parishioners and certainly lots of townspeople who were baffled and repulsed by him. Loretta was once asked by our physician, Dr. Hubbard, in his office: "Oh, don't you go to that church with that drunk crazy preacher?" We found his confirmation classes compelling and stimulating, nothing like the rote catechism study of my youth. After we were confirmed, I was almost immediately elected to the Vestry, where I served for the next seventeen or eighteen years, until Meredith was married with a child and decided to leave the church. Loretta and I continued at St. Andrew's for many years, and it was only after the retirement of my dear friend Father Jim Tuohy that I ceased to go with any kind of regularity.

I am an old man now, and I don't have much patience with the church. As I grow old and battle this arthritis and this dementia, I have little energy left for an institution that purports to exist for the good of all mankind yet is unable to come to any common policy of acceptance of people who were born with a different sexual orientation, that persists in believing that things sexual are at the heart of all sin. I believe that sin is willfully hurting other people in any myriad of ways; it is unkindness and backbiting and misrepresentation. Sin is greed and the accumulation of wealth while much of the world goes hungry. Jesus, the Christ who gave his name to the church, was extremely clear on this. I've spent forty years trying to change the church from the inside, and I'm tired. I admire my good friends and family who have the faith to continue to live their lives within the church. But my problem with the church is that—though I am a Christian—*I* could never find Christ in it.

That is very close to the way I feel about my country and my state. As a young man, I came hard up against the "Love it or leave it" mind-set. I came back to Alabama to teach and make my career and my home, because it *was* my home, and I did so in the belief that there was a third option to that love it or leave it idea, and that was to work for change, to make it better. I was raised in a segregated society, and I lived through the metamorphosis to a time when there were no more "separate but equal" schools, no more white-only drinking fountains and waiting rooms and lunch counters, a time when racial equality—though far from realized—became more than words on a page. I lived to a time when an African-American man could be elected president. That very idea fills me with pride in my country.

But I also know that I live in a country and especially a state still permeated with bigotry and racism, in which that president is hated for being an African-American, an "other." It saddens me after all these years, after all these struggles to throw off the George Wallace years and to move toward a fairer and more equitable way of life, that we are still mired in narrow-mindedness and ignorance. I wanted to do whatever I could to dent that stubborn resistance to reasonable intellectual inquiry that still prevails among the ultraconservative majority in this Bible Belt state. I always believed that reading and studying literature—especially that which challenges our comfortably held beliefs—is a good and positive thing. It is life affirming, in that it breeds understanding and tolerance. I think my stories and novels can contribute to understanding, empathy, and tolerance just as all serious literature does. I wanted to write good stories that people would enjoy because they were honest and real and true. I wanted my fiction to be empathic; I wanted readers to come to know my characters and situations—different from their own—and become briefly more fully alive as a result. To become close to someone who is different—for whatever reason—is to become more tolerant. I believe that strongly, and that belief has sustained me through a long life and career.

I moved to Livingston and enrolled at the college. I rented a large sunny room off the front porch of a big house near the courthouse square, downtown in Livingston. The house was owned by a widow named Mrs. Scales, who lived alone and seemed glad to have a young man there.

Robert Gilbert, the chairman of the English Department, was

a handsome young-middle age, a slight man with a ready, abrupt laugh, punctuated with a nod of his head. I enrolled in his course on the literature of the South. I was disappointed to learn that I had to take freshman English, even though I didn't consider myself on a degree track. I was put into a freshman history course as well. I didn't much care that I had already had a freshman history course. I was determined to make it count this time, to actually learn something.

It turned out that Dr. Gilbert taught the section of freshman English I was in, so I had him in two courses. In the freshman course we read short stories and wrote papers on them. In Southern lit, I began to read William Faulkner and discovered Flannery O'Connor that quarter. Dr. Gilbert was a gifted teacher, patient and clear in his analyses. It was as though the courses I'd had at Auburn had been in a different language. He treated me with respect, even asking from time to time about my writing. He told me he would soon teach a creative writing class and he wanted me to be in there.

The history class was taught by an ancient lady named Miss Hoover, who had taught there when my parents were in school. Her classes were hilarious, but she was demanding, giving tests that were far more detailed than any D. Roy Sharpe had given me. She always had a writing component to her tests. As I progressed through that first year, I realized that I was beginning to learn to write. It was as though I'd known all along how to do it; everything that Mrs. Gantt had drilled into my head came back to me in the doing of it. The best thing was that I was genuinely interested in the material. I felt comfortable and at home, as though I belonged. I went to my classes and took my meals at the café in the bus station near Mrs. Scales's house or at Rosenbush's Café downtown. I avoided places like the cafeteria and other places where students gathered. I felt older, more mature. I wasn't interested in fraternities and sororities, dating, doing the things that most college students wanted to do. My clothes were outdated and ratty; I wore Dickey's work shirts and stained, wrinkled khakis. Most of the other students seemed to me superficial, aping a kind of superconformity that I now rejected. They seemed amateurish with their keg parties; the group of bohemian students that I was forming friendships with drank and partied hard, and talked not about the football team but about art and literature.

I would sit out on the porch of Mrs. Scales's house and read all afternoon. I remember I read *The Sound and the Fury* for the first time then. I'd laugh out loud at some of Flannery O'Connor's stories. Mrs. Scales had gone off to visit one of her sons and I was all alone in the house, which was fine with me. I studied at night until late. I ate snacks in the room. I made an A in every one of my courses.

Mack Jordan came through with a part-time job at WXAL, which gave me enough money to live on and even pay my fees. I fell into a routine, driving to Demopolis after class on Friday to work a weekend shift at the radio station, working till close-up Friday night at eleven, back out there Saturday afternoon until sign-off that night. I opened up at five thirty Sunday morning and worked until noon, when I would drive back to Livingston. I usually spent Friday and Saturday nights with my folks. Sometimes Jayne would bring me my supper on Saturday night.

Then Byrd Burwell moved back to Demopolis from Chicago and also enrolled at Livingston. For the first time in my life, I fell in love. Byrd was in the high school class ahead of me, Winston's class, and though I knew her, we'd never run around together. Byrd had gone to Birmingham-Southern when Winston did and had dropped out to go to Chicago with a friend, where she worked at the National Conference of Christians and Jews. She had short, black hair and black eyes and wore horn-rimmed glasses. We started to hang out together on campus, and soon she was coming out to the radio station and sitting with me on Saturday nights.

Together we took Professor Nathaniel Reed's modern poetry course. Nat Reed was a younger professor with a degree from

Columbia. He was brilliant, a remarkable teacher. Byrd said he was as good as some of her professors at Birmingham-Southern, which enjoyed an excellent academic reputation. We were impressed that little Livingston had two professors of the caliber of Mr. Reed, whose specialty was medieval literature, and Dr. Gilbert. I managed, while I was there, to take every course the two of them offered. They gave me a first-class education. When I went to graduate school at Vanderbilt, I was as well prepared, or better, than my fellow graduate students, many of whom had gone to places like Brown, the University of Virginia, or North Carolina.

One day Nat Reed stopped me in the hallway and asked me if I was interested in moving into an apartment. He and his wife, Violet, who taught physical education, lived in a unique little cottage perched on the high bank of the Sucarnochee River, south of town. It was connected to the rustic house of a widow named Nelle Ennis. There was a small apartment attached to the cottage and it was vacant. The entire complex was in the woods and overlooked the river, a quiet, beautiful setting. It even had a garage for the Bullet.

The rent was more than I could afford on the money I was making. I had to get a roommate. Butch Ulmer, an English major and another one of Mrs. Gantt's former students, jumped at the chance to move out of the dorm and into the apartment with me. He was congenial, even tempered, stable, and a good cook. His mother always sent groceries with him when he came back from a visit home, including fresh beef from their farm. He liked bourbon and water and had excellent tastes in music. I had bought a small stereo, and he brought his album collection. I don't think we ever had a cross word the whole time we lived together. There was one bedroom with two single beds, one bathroom with a shower, a kitchen, and a living room. It was pretty far from the campus and he didn't have a car, but that was no problem. We could ride in together, and he could borrow the Bullet if he needed to.

The Reeds were fine neighbors. They had no children. They

had a huge gray cat named Grendel. They sometimes played badminton down along the riverbank and asked us to join them. We had many great, compelling conversations; Nat Reed was a trove of information about literature. Byrd and I spent as much time at the apartment as we could. Once her parents found out about it and her father was thoroughly pissed at me. Stomping around angry. I was shocked. After all, they had let her go off to Chicago.

Byrd and I became inseparable. She was as smart as Donald or Lester, and she taught me a great deal, especially about art and music. She introduced me to the works of Modigliani and Monet and the music of Leonard Bernstein. She was a painter, and she talked me into taking some art classes. We enrolled in Bill Tidwell's studio painting class together.

Bill Tidwell was another extraordinary man. He was an artist who exhibited widely, and a gentle, insightful teacher who seemed to spend all his time in his studio. I began to paint in oils and watercolor. (We still have one of my oil paintings hanging in our bedroom.) I also studied charcoal drawing with him. Byrd adored him. He took time with us and encouraged us to spend as much time in the studio as we liked.

We drank an awful lot, and partied frantically. We admired F. Scott and Zelda Fitzgerald, romancing their profligate lives, imagining that we, too, were doomed, beautiful artists. We were soon to be separated, with Byrd going back to Birmingham to reenroll and finish at Birmingham-Southern. On a couple of occasions I was able to get away and visit her, to meet her intellectual circle of friends there, active in theater and all the arts. And Byrd would ride the bus home on Friday, and I'd meet her in Demopolis. She'd spend the weekend with her folks and ride back to Livingston with me on Sunday, to catch the bus back to Birmingham.

Byrd graduated from Southern and took a job as a staff writer for *The Birmingham News*. She got a studio apartment on an upper floor of a high-rise on Highland Avenue, with a panoramic view of the city. Now I could go see her and spend the weekend. I worked out an arrangement where I could sometimes work at night during the week and have the weekend off. We had some wild parties in that apartment, with lots of Byrd's Birmingham-Southern friends and other writers from the *News*. We hung out at theatrical venues all over town, made the round of art galleries. Once we carried a collection of small watercolors of birds that Mr. Tidwell had done to an outdoor art festival downtown in Woodrow Wilson Park. We sold about twenty of them for him. We were living an iconoclastic, alcohol-soaked life.

One day not too many years ago, my father, with a smirk, handed me one of my old journals that he'd found in the attic. He quickly told me he'd read it. It covered the years I was at Livingston and into studio painting. I was struck by two things: (1) how often I wrote about how depressed I was, and (2) how much I was in love with Byrd.

Along about this time my father sent Jayne, my sister, to Auburn. He had not paid one penny for my higher education, claiming he could not afford it. Somehow he found the money to send Jayne and allow her to join a sorority. I think my depression at the time partly stemmed from this. I was doing okay; I liked Livingston. I hardly envied her being at Auburn, which I still regarded as a hellhole. But the disparity in treatment between the two of us was difficult for me. I felt rejected by my father, and that hurt me for the rest of my life. It was not until years later, after Loretta and I had been married ten years and we had bought a house, just after the Bread Loaf years, that I began to be treated for depression. I started to see a therapist regularly then, and I have been in some sort of therapy ever since.

Love was a new, exhilarating experience for me. It was intense. Byrd was passionate about art and life, and it was like I was coming alive and she was the midwife. I wrote stories, I wrote in my journal, I painted, I drank heavily. We went to movies in Birmingham, in the theaters that were still downtown then, sometimes to two films a day. Plays, the museum of art. We went to see Leonard

Bernstein and the New York Philharmonic, saw him conduct the overture from *Candide*, hair flying, met him at a reception that we were invited to by virtue of Byrd's press pass. I shook his hand. Some thirty years later, in 1987, his youngest son, Alexander Bernstein, would appear in *Sunday's Child*, my first play to be produced in New York. Byrd and I were leading a fast, heady existence, and there was no tomorrow.

Then there occurred an amazing development at Livingston: A kind of synchronistic merging of an incredible collection of students was suddenly in attendance, and they had all flunked out of other schools. There was Carmen Williams (Sweet Briar), Jim Connor (Harvard), Leslie Robinson (American Academy of Dramatic Art). We seemed to all attract each other like iron filings on a magnet, and our magnet was Robert Gilbert. We all took creative writing. We generated spontaneous creative energy just being together. We started a literary magazine: *The Sucarnochee Review*. Dr. Gilbert got us a supply of paper, use of a copying machine, and heavier paper for the cover. My first published short story, "The Year of Judson's Carnival," appeared in the maiden issue.

We all partied together. We were close, all of a like mind. Jim Connor rented a tumbled-down old house on the outskirts of town. We cooked out, drank beer. Dr. Gilbert joined us sometimes. Jim was an accomplished banjo player and singer, and we would gather at his house or my apartment and sing folk songs. Jim later was one half of the singing duo "Richard and Jim," recording several successful albums, and later still was for years a member of the Kingston Trio. We were the bohemians on campus. Some of us slyly instigated a food strike in the cafeteria—even though we didn't eat there—and we once picked up the dean of men and gave him a ride when we were all drunk out of our minds. We talked a country boy from way out in the sticks into running for president of the Student Government Association, campaigned for him, and he won.

I had taken a music appreciation course under a man named

Vernon Raines, who was also conductor of the Meridian, Mississippi, Symphony Orchestra. Mr. Raines approached me one day and asked me if I'd be interested in collaborating on a musical play of some kind. He had a student, Doug Cornell, who was a composer. Doug wanted to write a show and he needed someone to do the book and the lyrics.

We were aiming for some kind of performance the next spring. We didn't really know at first what we wanted it to be, but it gradually took shape as a book musical. I had always wanted to tell the story of Demopolis's founding as The Vine and Olive Colony, so I wrote a story about that, peopling it with characters both historically real and invented. I called it *The Vine And The Olive, a musical play in two acts*. As the undertaking grew, it generated considerable buzz on campus.

Dr. Gilbert was excited about it and prevailed on the administration to help us out by giving us a budget and allowing us to use the large auditorium in Bibb Graves Hall. All of my friends jumped in. Carmen Williams designed the set; her boyfriend, Shep Shepherd, put together a crew to build and paint it. Leslie Robinson designed the lighting, begging and borrowing lighting instruments and putting together a dimmer board, which the school did not have. Carmen also did the choreography. Everybody was in the play. Jim Connor was one of the stars. I directed and Doug Cornell was the music director.

The administration came across with funds to order costumes from a company in New York. We got statewide publicity when Byrd did a lengthy story for *The Birmingham News* weekly magazine supplement, with a big picture of me walking along the riverbank out at Riverside Cemetery, smoking my pipe, streamers of Spanish moss over my head. The caption read: "Author William Cobb, along the river where French Immigrants planted grape vines and olive trees." Byrd's present to me, at the play's opening, was a nice leather-bound album containing the story taped to the first page. Stamped in gold on the front was "William Cobb. Vol. I."

The play opened in early March and played for three performances over one weekend to SRO audiences. People streamed over from Demopolis to see it. Everyone was impressed with the professionalism of the production. I had gotten advice and help from some of Byrd's theater friends in Birmingham, and Leslie Robinson may have flunked out of the American Academy of Dramatic Art, but he seemed to know everything there was to know about theatrical productions. The orchestra, with students and members of the Meridian Symphony, was lively and full, and Doug's music was tuneful and soaring. The play was very funny. The audience whistled and applauded and gave us a standing ovation after each performance. I was called out on the stage to take a bow. It was a powerful moment: my first public recognition and praise for something I'd written.

My mother and father came over to see it. He told me afterward that he liked it and was proud of me. I had pleased him. I was successful at writing. I was also enjoying for a brief moment the only time I was ever a Big Man on Campus. I found out what it was like. For the first time in my life, girls threw themselves at me. My script girl on the play was a sexy little brunette cheerleader. We got along quite well. Years later, after I had given a reading and answered questions at the old courthouse in Monroeville, at an Alabama Writers' Symposium, an attractive late middle-aged woman stopped me with one of my books she wanted autographed. She smiled. She said softly, with a twinkle: "I started to raise my hand and ask if I was the only one in the room who'd had sex with William Cobb."

When I had started at Livingston, I'd had no intention of ever graduating. I was just taking courses, whatever I wanted to take. Art, music, ballroom dancing because there were pretty girls in there. Dean Ralph Lyon, a gruff and crusty man, called me in one day and told me I had been there almost five years and I needed to think about finishing. He had my transcript on the desk in front of him. He told me I had far more hours than I needed. He informed me wryly that I had already completed a major in English, one in history, with two minors, political science and art. He seemed somewhat confused about my intentions. "Don't you want to graduate?" he asked me, his bushy gray eyebrows wiggling. I still lacked some basic requirements: a freshman biology class, a math class, a general education introduction to psychology.

Dr. Gilbert advised me to complete those requirements and apply to graduate school. I had made all A's at Livingston, but those courses at Auburn were still on my record, which lowered my point average somewhat. Dr. Gilbert wrote letters of recommendation and we applied for every fellowship and scholarship we could find. Vanderbilt seemed eager to admit me, but not so much they'd give me any help. I would have to find some kind of job in Nashville and borrow money to get through, but I was willing to do it.

I had made up my mind that I wanted to teach literature and creative writing in college. I was not confident enough in my abilities to just go off and be a writer. I needed a way to earn a living that would leave me some time to write. Dr. Gilbert agreed with me that college teaching was the answer. I loved books and literature and wanted to spend my life with them. I had become confident enough to know what I wanted to do with my life.

Ten

My old friend from childhood, Winston Smith, was in the graduate program at Vanderbilt on a Woodrow Wilson Fellowship. He was a friend of Byrd's, and when he was home in Demopolis or visiting in Birmingham, we'd get together. Winston and I had always liked each other immensely and now found that we had more common ground than ever. We had the same sense of humor. We both thought that Faulkner's Snopeses were the funniest bunch of characters ever created and we swapped stories about colorful people we'd known or heard of around Demopolis, like Joe Bynymo, Greensboro, Rhett Brown, Bud Legare, and Edwina Wilson. He encouraged me to write about them.

Winston asked me if I wanted to share an apartment in Nashville. Dr. Gilbert had helped me arrange student loans, so I had some cash to tide me over for a while. We drove up to Nashville in Winston's beat-up old station wagon and looked for an apartment. It was the first time I'd been back in Nashville; it didn't seem to have changed any. We found a small one-bedroom garret apartment on the top floor of a brownstone on 21st Street, across from the Peabody campus, about six blocks south of the Joint University Libraries, a half block from the little Krystal where I'd worked five years earlier. It was furnished with a double bed, but that was no problem, since there was a daybed in the living room that Winston claimed for his, since he liked to watch television late into the night and it wouldn't disturb me. And it would be a fine arrangement for when Byrd wanted to visit. The bathroom was off the living room, and the kitchen was at the front with a window overlooking 21st Street, Hillsboro Road. Out that window I watched John F. Kennedy go by in an open car in a motorcade. He was so close it seemed I could have reached out and touched him.

Donald was at King's College, Cambridge. His letters were profane and colorful, funny and intellectually stimulating. I got long letters from Pat as well. He had finished basic training at Parris Island, South Carolina, as the top recruit in his class and, as a result, had been offered his choice of duty anywhere in the world, including embassy duty in Europe and Asia. Pat chose a lengthy assignment guarding a nuclear ammunition dump in the desert near Hawthorne, Nevada. It was quiet, he wrote me, undemanding, and he would have plenty of time to write. He planned to finish a novel. Donald wrote that he was on the editorial board of a new literary magazine called *Granta*. They were doing an American issue and he solicited a short story from me. My second published story, "The Time of the Leaves," appeared there.

I sold my car to give me more cash. We would be within walking distance of the campus, and if I needed to get around in the city, I could use the busses. And Winston had a car. We got settled in at the apartment on Hillsboro Road. Winston was great fun to live with. He was droll and jocular, and we spent a lot of our time laughing, just as we always had. He had purchased a little black-and-white television set, and after his studying at night, he would begin watching when the *Jack Parr Show* came on and watch all night. He would stretch out on the daybed wearing a ratty old terry cloth robe. Sometimes we watched earlier, like the

Friday night fights. We would go to a Shoney's Big Boy over near Belmont College, get a sack full of double cheeseburgers, stop at a mini-market and get several large three-liter bottles of beer. Once or twice a week we cooked: hamburgers, or sale-priced steaks from the supermarket at Hillsboro Village.

My first semester I took a Southern literature seminar with Dr. Randall Stewart—who was the chair of the English Department—and a creative writing workshop under Donald Davidson. Dr. Stewart was a renowned critic of American literature, author of the seminal text *American Literature and Christian Doctrine*. He had retired as chair at Brown and had come to Vandy. He was the editor of the textbook we had used in Dr. Gilbert's course my first quarter at Livingston. Donald Davidson had published several volumes of poems and criticism. He was the last of the "Fugitives," a distinguished group of poets and critics at Vanderbilt in the late twenties and early thirties. Others in the group were Robert Penn Warren, John Crowe Ransom, and Allen Tate. Ransom came back for a semester while I was there and lived in a brownstone across the street. I would see him, a tiny gray-haired man, in the grocery store. I always sneaked a look in his basket to see what a Pulitzer Prize–winning poet ate. He usually had cans of Campbell's Vegetable Soup and a package of fig newtons.

The classes met in Old Central, an old stone farmhouse in the middle of the campus, Mr. Davidson's in his spacious office on the second floor, Dr. Stewart's in a large room on the first floor called "The Fugitive Room," a sort of commons with sofas and comfortable chairs and a seminar table. On the wall were pictures of all the men and a plaque reading, HERE DAILY PASSED THE FUGITIVES.

Both men were quite old. Dr. Stewart was a tweedy little gray-haired man who spoke with a slow drawl. He kept a bottle of bourbon, a cocktail glass, a sugar bowl and spoon, and a pitcher of water on the windowsill in his office for toddies throughout the day. He had a red bulb nose and wore an Irish plaid wool hat. Mr. Davidson was a serious man with a severe demeanor; he had penetrating little eyes behind thick spectacles. He wore three-button blue serge suits that looked as if they were left over from 1920. All the graduate students were scared to death of him. He drove a black Cadillac about half a block long, which he'd been parking on campus for decades; when the administration closed the campus to cars and shut down all the parking spaces, Mr. Davidson simply drove through the gate and parked on the lawn in front of Old Central.

There were other, younger professors, of course. Vanderbilt was a vital, exciting, challenging place to be; the English department had a sterling national reputation. Walter Sullivan, a young novelist, taught fiction writing. My fellow graduate students were an interesting and stimulating bunch of people from all over the country. It was the most intellectually charged atmosphere I'd ever been in. We lived for literature and writing. The coffee shops and bars around the campus vibrated with our earnest dialogues and arguments.

Byrd and I grew apart. We had talked about marriage, but I was not conventional enough for that. Our relationship did not survive another long separation. We wrote for a while. Neither of us had a car, and it would have meant long bus rides to visit back and forth. There was a young man in her building, in the next apartment, named John Rish. I knew him and liked him, and I had sensed an attraction between them. The next thing I knew, Byrd had married him, and that was that. They are still married and have grown children, and I've seen her occasionally and even exchanged e-mails. We remain friends. I think we both value what we had together. I certainly do.

I loved my courses. I knew I was learning a great deal. Mr. Davidson seemed fond of me and was encouraging about my work. That first semester I wrote the first draft of a long, almost novella-length story I called "The Stone Soldier," set in Demopolis in the years right after the Civil War. Mr. Davidson liked it so much he sent it to one of his former students, the writer Jesse Stuart, who wrote me a long letter of encouragement. Jesse Stuart made some suggestions for improvement, and I set about making them. "The Stone Soldier" was later published in *Story* magazine and now forms the first story in my collection *Sweet Home: Stories of Alabama*.

The second semester I took Mr. Davidson's course on the English lyric. Mostly undergraduate, it was a popular course and was packed. The seven graduate students sat in the front of the room. The syllabus covered the development of the lyric poem in England from the medieval street ballads up to the poetry of William Butler Yeats. Mr. Davidson brought his guitar and sang many of the ballads to us. It was fascinating. That class was notable because it contained the first African-American student to attend Vanderbilt. She was a graduate student at Fisk University, across town. When Mr. Davidson asked if anyone in the class read "Old French," she was the only one who raised her hand.

Donald Davidson would retire the next year, and I was the last student he directed. After much persuading on my part, he agreed to let me write a collection of short stories for my master's thesis, something that had never been done before at Vanderbilt. He felt that a thesis should be scholarly, not creative. He was a very conservative man, a throwback to an earlier period (he sincerely thought we should all be studying Latin and Greek), so he told me that though he recommended that I be allowed to do it, I would have to get Walter Sullivan to approve and sign off on the final manuscript, though I had written many of the stories in his classes. I was taking Walter's "Modern British and American Fiction," and he agreed to direct the thesis. (I admired his novel *The Long, Long Love*.)

In the middle of the first year, I realized that I'd not be able to make it unless I found a job. It would have to be something in the evenings or at night, as I had classes during the day. I called a couple of the smaller radio stations, but there were no openings. I heard that Third National Bank, downtown on 3rd Avenue and

Church, had night shifts in their bookkeeping and transit departments and that other students worked there. (At that time there were fourteen institutions of higher learning in Nashville, so there were a lot of students.) I went down and applied. I got the job.

Before I started work, Winston and I went down to Oxford, Mississippi, with the vague intention of seeing William Faulkner. (I later wrote an article about this incident called "Looking for Mr. Faulkner." It appeared in the March 1987 issue of *Southern Living Magazine.*) We had no idea if we'd get to see him or not, but we were determined to try. We located his house, only to see that the yard was posted. We found him in the phone book and called the house. Mrs. Faulkner answered. She told us that "Bill" was working and would not see anybody, but we'd be welcome to come out to Rowan Oak and look around. We did. We encountered Mrs. Faulkner, sitting on a side veranda, sipping bourbon from a teacup. She spoke to us and told us to wander around all we wanted, to make ourselves at home. I was standing at the corner of the house, Winston out in the yard to make my picture, when Faulkner walked around the side of the house and ran right into me. I was flabbergasted and tongue-tied. He glared at me with his coal black eyes. He was a little man, not even as tall as me, with salt-and-pepper hair. Then he smiled and winked and walked off down to the edge of the lawn and stood smoking his pipe. I was not about to talk to the great man, and Winston wasn't either. He was a notoriously private person. The best we had the courage to do was snap his picture. We totally missed our chance, since he died within the year.

I started my job at Third National Bank. I went to work at 10 p.m. and worked until 3 a.m. five nights a week. I started out in the transit department. I ran a huge machine that sorted checks for distribution all over the Southeast. (Nashville was a financial hub.) It was boring work, standing feeding stacks of checks into the machine, but the pay was good, better, I think, than any other part-time job I could have found. Most of the people working there were young, mostly male, though there were some fetching girls who got a lot of attention. There was a lot of horseplay. I fell in with a group of guys who would go for our midnight lunch break to a little German café called The Gerst House, on 1st Avenue near the river bridge. We'd walk through Printer's Alley and look in the strip clubs, then sit in The Gerst House and eat Berliner Mit Sausages with Sauerkraut (a heaping plate that cost 50 cents) and, though we weren't supposed to, drink beer that came in huge steins like fishbowls.

In that group was a tall, thin young man named Robert Street, or Bobby. He had a waggish sense of humor and I liked him immensely. We soon became close friends. Bobby was the son of Claude Street, who owned and ran C. P. Street Piano Company, a longtime and prominent Nashville business. He was a student at Peabody, though he didn't seem to be a serious one. He lived at home with his parents. Bobby had been an actor. He had recently come home from Traverse City, Michigan, where he had played Eugene Gantt in a summer stock production of *Look Homeward, Angel*. He told me he didn't want to pursue a theatrical career. He worked some for his father, took a few classes, and worked at Third National. Sometimes we'd go back to The Gerst House after work or to other bars around town. Bobby would take me home in one of his father's big piano delivery vans that he drove around town.

Toward the end of my first year of study, Winston told me he'd decided to move on campus into housing provided for teaching fellows, a position he would hold the next fall. I asked Bobby if he'd be interested in sharing an apartment, and he said he would. So we made plans for him to move into the apartment with me.

I had gotten to know some of Bobby Street's friends. Two of them were the couple Clem and Eleanor Dore. Clem, who taught philosophy at Vanderbilt, was an exceptionally brilliant man who could talk interestingly at length on seemingly any subject. Eleanor was dark haired, alluring, and charming. Their home had a salon-like atmosphere, with many gatherings and parties. They liked their whiskey, especially Clem, who could match me drink for drink. Eleanor was a wonderful cook, sometimes cooking dishes like roast leg of lamb for large groups of drunken people.

Two of the people I met at the Dores' were a young married couple, Joyce and Bobby Paul, who lived in a ground-floor apartment in the building where I lived. It was a much nicer apartment than ours, with a tile floor, a door that opened onto the sidewalk at street level, a large bedroom with two beds, a living room, and a kitchen. They told me they were moving into a house and the place would soon be vacant. They paid about the same rent we were paying. So Bobby and I rented it, and when Winston went home for the summer in June, we moved in.

Bobby was teaching himself to play the banjo. I had my typewriter set up in the bedroom, and over the summer I worked on a novel. (I eventually finished it. It was not very good. It was fairly derivative of *The Sun Also Rises.* It was based on a trip my Livingston crowd took down to Carmen Williams's parents' fabulous place in Magnolia Springs, down near the Gulf, where we drank prodigious amounts of liquor and played musical beds. It was entitled *The Doves Came Straightway Flying.* I took the title from John Crowe Ransom's poem "The Equilibrists.")

Pat Brasfield came home from the Marine Corps and he and Jayne became engaged. They were to be married in the Presbyterian Church in Demopolis, and Pat wanted me to be best man at the wedding. I had to ride the bus home for a long weekend to be in the festivities. I don't think my mother was any too happy about the match, especially when she found out that Pat wanted to go back to Nevada after they married, to enroll at the University of Nevada in Reno. He wanted to study writing with Walter Van Tilburg Clark there. Jayne and Pat would be in Reno for four years, with Pat attending school and Jayne working in a bank.

Bobby and I were both now working in the bookkeeping department, a much better job, a promotion with more money. This was in the pre-computer era, when customers' accounts had to be posted by hand. We worked in a huge room with several rows of posting machines. They had keyboards, and the transactions were imprinted on the account sheets as they slid through. Most of us were fast, our fingers flying over the keys as the checks and deposit slips popped up in front of us. We raced to see who could finish first. You had to be good, since the accounts had to be reconciled at the end of the shift and correcting errors counted against you. It was hard work, but it was fun. Even though I worked long hours (especially around the first of the month), I managed to keep up with my classes. I just didn't get much sleep.

Our apartment was always full of friends. For a while Bobby and I kept a keg of beer in the kitchen so we could offer draft beer. We had poker games for the guys at the bank. Every Sunday we'd go out to Bobby's parents' house for lunch. We'd sit and drink sherry before going to the table. A young Vanderbilt professor, Hal Weatherby, was usually there; he was a friend of Bobby's older brother Parke, who was an Episcopal priest in Louisville. In May, Bobby and I went to visit Parke in Louisville for the Kentucky Derby; we got drunk in the infield and didn't see much of the race.

Bobby quit at the bank and went to work full-time for his father, selling electric organs to churches. We continued to live together on Hillsboro. I began to think seriously about finding a teaching job. Mr. Davidson warned me that I would probably be able to get a job with just a master's (he was writing me glowing recommendations), but without a PhD, I would have difficulty getting promoted and getting tenure. I was shocked to learn that he, himself, had had to struggle to get promoted at Vanderbilt, with his reputation and publications, because he did not have a terminal degree. I knew I was not a scholar, I was a writer, but I had a lot to offer students, just as he did.

I sent out a lot of letters. LSU wrote back that they would be happy to have me in their PhD program. The chairman of the department at Austin Peay wrote that though I was the kind of young person they were looking for, they had no openings at that time.

I was invited to come to Middle Tennessee State in Murphreesboro for an interview. There was a big basement room with rows of desks for instructors, who were teaching five freshman composition courses each semester. They offered me a job. It was close to Nashville, and I wouldn't have to leave all my friends there. I was tempted.

Dr. Gilbert had told me that if I wanted to come back to Alabama to teach, I should apply to Alabama College in Montevallo. Alabama College was a small liberal arts school that for years had been the state college for women. The chairman of the English department was a Vanderbilt PhD, John Lott. I had sent him an inquiry, but I hadn't heard anything. One day I got a letter from him asking me if I was still interested. He asked me to call him if I was. I called him on a pay phone and we agreed that I would come for an interview. He said they would fly me down to Birmingham and meet me at the airport.

Other than when I flew over Demopolis with Mack Jordan in his Piper Cub, it was the first plane ride I ever took. (I never let on to that fact once I was in Montevallo.) I flew from Nashville to Atlanta on a prop plane that looked like the one in *Casablanca*, changed planes, and flew on to Birmingham.

John Lott was a tall, thin angular man with a slightly effeminate way of wringing his hands, entwining his long fingers. He was only a few years older than I was. I liked him immediately. Before we left the airport to drive the twenty-five miles to Montevallo, I already knew that this was no Murphreesboro. The campus looked like a private school, with a greensward, stately trees, flowering shrubs, and brick streets that gave it a cobblestoned look out of another era. The English Department was on the second floor of Comer Hall, an aging, timeworn building with cramped offices. I was introduced around.

Since the college had only recently gone coed, most of the senior professors were women. There was Dr. Eva Golson, a rosy-cheeked lady with a knitted white fascinator on her head, tied under her chin with a bow. Sara Puryear, a delightful woman with a quick laugh. Eloise Meroney, an imposing lady with steely eyes that reminded me of Mr. Davidson's. Dr. Lott and I sat in his office at the end of the hall. He told me he wanted to start offering a junior-level course in creative writing. My teaching experience was zero, but I assured him that I could teach it. "Yes," he said, "Mr. Davidson said you could." I would teach two sections of freshman English, one of sophomore survey, and creative writing. The pay would be $5,000 a year. I told him I would take it, we shook hands, and I flew back to Nashville.

Eleven

When our daughter, Meredith, was born, I had been dry for about a year. I knew I had a drinking problem, and I knew I'd have to do something about it eventually. At least I knew that intellectually. I didn't know it in my gut. I had simply stopped drinking, cold turkey.

I was pretty proud of myself; this time I told myself that I'd finally licked it. But there was some reserve, some emotional commitment held back. I could not really face up to the prospect that I'd never, for the rest of my life, have another drink. The booze would always be there. It was sort of like my father when he quit smoking. He'd been a heavy smoker all his adult life, and when he quit, he carried a pack with one cigarette in his shirt pocket in case he ever decided to smoke again. When he had gone long enough that he knew he'd kicked the habit, he threw it away. My father had discovered the principle of "one day at a time" without labeling it.

Loretta had gotten pregnant the first time the previous year and we were very happy. Two months into her term she began to experience pain in her abdomen and abnormal bleeding. I drove her into Birmingham to see her OB-GYN, who thought there was nothing to be alarmed about. We came home. The pains got worse. She could barely get out of the bed. We called our faithful old doctor, Dr. Hubbard, who came to the house and examined her. He told us to go back into town and see her doctor there. While Loretta was being examined in the office, she began to feel faint. Her doctor, realizing that something was seriously wrong, had her admitted to St. Vincent's Hospital, which was just adjacent to his office. It was an ectopic pregnancy. Her tube had ruptured in the office, and she underwent immediate emergency surgery. Had we not been that close to the hospital, she might well have died.

The loss of the child was devastating to us both, especially to Loretta. She wanted a child with a fierceness and determination that was typical of her. It was a monumental setback. I had been controlling my drinking, but even before she came home from the hospital, I was hitting it pretty hard again. When I brought her home, we were disconsolate. We were both depressed. As time passed, she grew less and less moody and morose. After several months she was her old self. But she still insisted that she knew the tiny baby was a boy. She had calculated and she knew what would have been his birth date. The doctor was unsure whether we could, or should, get pregnant again. She now had only one fallopian tube. We knew we didn't want to adopt. We had many long talks; we decided that we were child-*free*, not child*less*.

After one particular long weekend of drinking, I vowed to quit, and I did. I wanted a new life for us. I was working well; I had published a few short stories and I was working on a novel about a naive girl who comes to Nashville from a little country town. It was a comic story full of colorful characters. It was episodic, describing all her adventures. I had converted the back bedroom of our house into a studio and I worked regularly and steadily on the novel. I felt good physically. Loretta regained her strength and went back to work. My teaching was going well; I was enjoying my classes.

Time began to pass easily and gently; our routine was comfortable and renewed.

Then Loretta got pregnant again. We were ecstatic, but cautious. We didn't want to tell anyone. Both our sets of parents—though they had other grandchildren—had been terribly disappointed when we lost the first child. Loretta and I had been through all sorts of fertility treatments and exercises before the first pregnancy, and since then, in our new resolve, with my "sobriety" that I refused to believe was delusional, we had started to investigate adoption. We were almost to the point of making the official applications when she became pregnant.

We were in a period of sublime contentment, as happy as either one of us had been in our lives. The church was a comfort to us. We had good friends, people we loved, who loved us, and we felt safe and sheltered. We loved our house; we had lived in a series of apartments since we'd been married, and we'd bought a big old drafty rambling house outside of town in a grove of pine trees, on a dirt road.

I was pleased with my progress on my novel and showed the beginnings to Donald. Donald and his first wife had gotten a divorce and he had married again. He had bought an old warehouse building in lower Manhattan and converted it into loft apartments. It was in Soho, on the edge of Little Italy, near Chinatown, where lots of artists and writers were moving. Donald lived on the top floor in the biggest loft, with hardwood floors and skylights and windows overlooking Grand Street. Donald had recently signed on with a new agency, Al Zuckerman's Writers House. Donald showed him my manuscript and he liked it and agreed to represent it.

I flew up there over Labor Day weekend and stayed with Don and Dianne. Don and I drove out to Al's house on Long Island for drinks and steaks on the holiday. Al was a likable, pleasant man. We took to each other immediately. His cramped office was over a porn movie theater just off Times Square (you could hear the faint sounds of lust coming up through the floor). He was enthusiastic and eager to place my novel when I finished it. We shook hands on it.

Susan Meredith Cobb was born on October 7, 1974. The name *Susan* was after my mother. *Meredith* was for William Meredith, the poet we had met and come to know at Bread Loaf and who had become a dear friend. She was born at St. Vincent's Hospital. When Loretta's contractions began, we drove up to spend the night with one of Loretta's good friends and one of my former students, Sandra King Ray and her family. They lived in Homewood, near the hospital, and we didn't want to take any chances. She is now Cassandra King, an accomplished writer. She's married to the novelist Pat Conroy. They remain good friends of ours to this day.

I started that first year teaching three freshman sections of composition and my creative writing workshop. I had never taught before, and I had to learn by doing. Sandra King was one of the first writing students I had, in my first writing workshop. She was good friends with an attractive girl named Loretta Douglas, whom I was going to get to know quite well.

My apartment in Montevallo was tiny. It was one of three on the second floor of a red brick building just off the campus, an easy walk from Comer Hall, where my office was. It was furnished with a three-quarters bed, and there was a huge desk in the small living room for my typewriter. It had an upholstered easy chair with an ottoman next to the windows. It had no shower, which took some adjusting since I hadn't taken tub baths since I lived at home in high school.

The amount of money I owed for graduate school was daunting. I had a long time to pay it back and some of it was government loans that would be partially forgiven if I taught in a public school. I didn't worry about it. Money had always meant very little to me, as long as I had the necessities: food and booze and a place to lay my head.

I was excited that I'd finally be making enough money to relax, but when I came home after I graduated, I was dead-ass broke. I was not scheduled to begin teaching until the fall, so I needed something lucrative to do. I got a job at Gulf States Paper Company in Demopolis for the summer, doing fill-in work for people who were going on vacation. My father and my Uncle Oscar came to Nashville to take me and my meager belongings home. They checked into a motel and took me and Bobby Street out to dinner. We all got drunk. We took them to a bar we liked, to listen to a blind black piano player named Sonny. Bobby could not believe how much my father and Uncle Oscar drank.

The next morning we packed up the car and headed home. I was in the backseat surrounded by my stuff (my clothes, typewriter, a few kitchen utensils), Uncle Oscar in the passenger seat and my father driving. We hadn't made it farther south than Franklin when my Uncle turned to the backseat and said, "Billy, your daddy's driving along real nicely, it's a real pretty day, and it's time we all had a drink, so pour us some bourbon back there." It was only nine o'clock or so. I made us a drink, and we drank liquor all the way home. We dropped Uncle Oscar off in Uniontown and continued on to Demopolis. My mother was none too happy with us when we arrived.

Don't ever let anybody tell you that you can't smell a paper mill if you're working inside it. It's like spending your day in an outhouse where somebody has just had violent diarrhea. You can't get away from it. I was assigned to the lab on the graveyard shift, eleven to seven, just like the Krystal. I wore a khaki shirt with a red collar. My job was to keep tabs on the effluent so the mill wouldn't send too much toxic shit into the river and kill all the fish. I had to ride a bicycle all over the plant, consisting of numerous buildings that covered several acres, and take samples at various stages of the process of paper making. I would take them back to the lab and run tests on them. I also had to drive a jeep down to Rooster Bridge, five miles below the plant, to take a sample of water from the river. I had to do that twice a shift. (I liked that, going down to the river by myself in the middle of the night.) I had to take a sample from a foul-smelling vat called "the sump," and get one where the settling ponds drained into the river. It was a nasty job.

I slept most of every day. I bought a new car from my father, a sporty little burgundy LeMans with four in the floor. My mother was working at Frohsins' Department Store, so I bought some new clothes with her discount. I would need them to teach in. I was able to save a good bit of money, so I had quite a stash at the end of the summer.

Before school was to start, my folks and I took a driving trip out to Reno to see Jayne and Pat. We stopped in Las Vegas for a couple of nights. (I sent a postcard back to the guys in the lab. It had a picture of the Strip, with all the glittering lights. I wrote, "The Sump is Overflowing!") We went on to Reno. Jayne and Pat had a two-bedroom apartment, so I slept on the sofa. My father and mother played a lot of slot machines. Pat and I played blackjack. Jayne was working. You could get free liquor while you gambled, of course, so we drank all day every day. We went to topless shows, and drove out to Hoover Dam. After a week, my folks and I drove on over to San Francisco, then down the coast to Los Angeles. We drove around looking at stars' houses. We took the southern route home, going into Mexico at Nuevo Laredo.

I was assigned an office up on the third floor, a narrow room that I was to share with another instructor, who was beginning her second year of teaching. I had asked John Lott if I could drop the sophomore survey (world literature) and take another freshman composition class, and he had agreed. I had three classes with about twenty students in each. My creative writing class had ten students. I wore a coat and tie every day. I met another young instructor in the history department, Reuben Triplett, and we quickly became drinking buddies. He was friends with another hard-drinking couple in the history department, Jesse and Shirley Jackson. The three of them provided me with some social life. They were fun party animals, and we'd sit up all night playing "B for Botticelli." They were extremely conservative; it was the Goldwater year and they were on fire with him. They had not mourned the death of John Kennedy, which annoyed me. They gave me books to read, one entitled *A Texan Looks at Lyndon*, that I could quickly see was pure bullshit. I was apolitical. I just didn't think too much about that sort of stuff. I had never voted, was not even registered.

I had listened to radio reports (I had no television) of the 16th St. Baptist Church bombing in Birmingham. I read the newspaper reports of the marches, the police dogs, and the fire hoses. The news of those events was strangely muted; I think they were much more widely known outside Alabama than within. It was all only thirty miles up the road, yet it seemed distant. It didn't seem to be touching my life. It wouldn't until I went down to Selma before the voting rights march to Montgomery the next year. I was curious. I drove down there and went out to Brown Chapel AME Church, the headquarters of the Selma march. I visited with all the people, talked with them. It was eye-opening for me. I would later use much of this experience in my novel *Wings of Morning.*

One day, unexpectedly (I had forgotten all about it), I got a letter from Whit Burnett, the editor of *Story* magazine in New York, informing me that I had been awarded first prize in that year's short story contest. Mr. Davidson and I, months before, had entered my story "The Stone Solder" in the competition; we had seen an ad in a literary magazine. The story would appear in the next issue of *Story* and would be the title story in a volume of prize stories to be published in the spring. The prize was $500.

John Lott and the administration were pleased. *Story* wanted me to come to New York for interviews and appearances. The college quickly made arrangements to fly me up there. Whit Burnett met me at Idlewild and took me to the Overseas Press Club, where

I was to stay. Mr. Burnett was a dapper man with a chopped gray mustache. He had been editor of *Story* for years and had published the first stories of Norman Mailer and J. D. Salinger. He had edited numerous anthologies of short fiction and would edit *The Stone Soldier: Prize Winning Stories.* He and his wife, the novelist Hallie Burnett, an elegant, exquisite lady, had me to dinner. There was a reception at the Overseas Press Club for critics from around the country, and I was interviewed on television. I went out with a bunch of other writers and managed to get very drunk, but they all did, too.

My return flight had not been in the air more than half an hour when the pilot came on and announced that we were experiencing some difficulties and were returning to New York. Something had jammed on the wing flaps and made them inoperable. Since the landing in New York might be a rough one, we were circling out over the Atlantic to drop fuel to prevent a fire. The atmosphere in the cabin was understandably tense. There was praying, cursing, and crying. Fortunately that was back in the days when complimentary drinks were served on all flights, even domestic ones, so I was able to anesthetize myself. They had us put pillows on our laps and put our heads down. We landed with much bumping and swaying. When we stopped, I looked out the window. We were surrounded by fire trucks and ambulances, all with flashing lights.

The inside of the terminal was chaotic. Everyone was trying to get connections. It seemed to take me forever, but I finally got on a flight to Atlanta. It was fairly uneventful until we were near Atlanta when we ran into a massive thunderstorm. We bumped and rolled all the way in. The airport was closing because of the weather, and I was on the last flight that was allowed to land. No flights would leave before the next day. I was put into a hotel near the airport. I arrived back in Birmingham the following afternoon.

Twelve

John Lott allowed me to add two new upper-division courses, "The Modern Novel" and "Southern Literature." In those mid-sixties years, there was an exceptional group of English majors at Montevallo, and I was truly enjoying my work. I was teaching what I wanted to teach, the writers and books I chose, and I felt that I was leading the literary life I had desired and dreamed about. I liked my colleagues. I was moved down to the second floor to a larger office that I shared with Charlotte Blackmon, an intelligent, delightful woman a little older than me.

Sandra King's friend, Loretta Douglas, was a work-study student that I noticed around the office. She was a petite blonde with a perfect oval face and eyes so green they'd excite a gemologist. She had full, soft-looking lips, fair skin, a youthful shape. She would come into my office and sit and flirt with me. I had gotten used to coeds' flirtations (not so much I didn't still enjoy them), but this one was different. She had a quiet confidence about her that was alluring. And I could tell she was smart.

She enrolled in my modern novel course and sat on the front

row. She sat next to Sandra King. They both had long slim legs and wore miniskirts. Miss Douglas was often not present when I called the roll. I would look out the window (the class was on the first floor) and see her walking, ambling really, down the brick sidewalk from the dorm. Though the chimes had rung, she was obviously in no hurry. I would wait to begin my lecture until she came into the room and floated gracefully into her desk. "We can begin now," I would say, "Miss Douglas is here." She would smile and cross her legs. She told me later that Sandra had told her to cross her legs a lot in my class, that I liked to look.

I began to see her around campus. I'd run into her at foreign films that were showing in Comer Auditorium that semester. Once, on a Saturday, I saw her sitting with friends on the steps in front of the library and stopped to chat. I sat with her and some of her friends at a downtown dive called the Pizza Villa and ate pizza. I saw her at a street dance. There was a couple really getting with it, a writhing slow dance, and she, standing next to me said, "Look, Mr. Cobb, they're practically *doing it*."

Eudora Welty was coming to Tuscaloosa to give a reading. Reuben Triplett and I were going over there, so we invited three girls to go with us: Joanne Lancaster, an honors English major; Martha Helen Hubbard, the editor of the student newspaper *The Alabamian*; and Loretta Douglas. We had dinner on the way home at a barbeque joint in Centerville. I was realizing that I liked this girl quite a lot. Jesse and Shirley liked her, too, and they thought I should go out with her. But I wasn't sure I wanted to date a student. And she was in my class.

The department took some students to Oxford, Mississippi, to the Southern Literary Festival, and Loretta went along. (She later wrote of this incident in her story "The Darling Buds of May," in her collection *The Ocean Was Salt*.) We took walks together when she got off work. We often sat on a bench on campus and talked until after dark. It seemed natural that we kiss. Once I asked her to ride up to Oak Mountain State Park on a Saturday. We took a bottle of wine and a blanket and lay on the side of the mountain and watched the clouds. She asked me if I wanted to see her bra, something new called a "nude bra," a sort of net in flesh tones with ribbons; I sat with my mouth hanging open in shock as she opened her blouse, pulled her blouse aside, and flashed me. She laughed gaily, flopping back on the blanket. Her emerald eyes were sparkling in the sunshine, her silky hair glistening.

Since she was in my class, it was probably not a good thing to be dating her, but I didn't give a damn by then. I knew I wanted to be with Loretta Douglas. We had a date and went to the drive-in movie (*Sweet Bird of Youth*, I remember, though I didn't see much of the picture). She walked from the dorm and met me at my car, and when I took her back to the dorm, we created quite a stir. I pulled up and there were hundreds of couples standing around (there was a curfew back then; all the girls had to be in by eleven) and Loretta was going to get out quietly and run inside. When she opened the door, several empty beer cans fell out on the brick street and raised a clatter. I heard some boy say, "Hey, that's Mr. Cobb!" Everybody was looking, pointing.

We were both relieved when the semester ended and Loretta got a job at Internal Revenue in downtown Birmingham for the summer. She would live with her sister and her husband out in Woodlawn. We would be able to date freely, without attracting stares. I was teaching summer school, but managed to get into Birmingham every weekend. By the middle of the summer, she moved into a room at the YWCA downtown.

We marveled at how much we had in common. We had both worked our first jobs in movie theaters. She was working her way through college, just as I had. I was seven years older than she was, but it didn't seem to make any difference at all. We went to see movies and loved the same ones. She was an English major and loved literature. We liked the same writers. She wanted to write. I thought we were made for each other, that she had somehow been heaven-sent to me. She was so natural, so at ease. I made up my mind. I was in love. I had known her less than six months, but I was sure she was the girl I wanted to marry and live with for the rest of my life. (Fifty years later I can say with certainty that I was right.)

One morning, over breakfast in a café, we talked about it. She felt the same way, but she didn't trust her instincts as much as I did mine. We talked about how awkward it would be in the fall when school started back, how we'd be going through the same old crap all over again. I said maybe we ought to get married. She was nibbling on a carrot stick. (She had ordered a salad and a Coke for breakfast.) She didn't have to think very long before she agreed that we probably ought to do it. I didn't have a ring. (I had not planned to do this.) She told me it didn't matter. All she wanted was a simple gold band.

We went up to Pell City for me to meet her stepfather and mother and tell them what we were planning. Loretta's father drove a produce truck. They had a roadside produce business on the highway and lived in a small house behind it. Neither one of them had ever been to college, so they were visibly surprised that she was marrying a professor, one that already had some gray hair. But they seemed pleased. The next weekend we drove down to Demopolis for Loretta to meet my folks. I had not prepared them ahead of time, but I could tell they knew. My parents liked Loretta immediately. They seemed relieved that I was finally settling down. They were happy that I hadn't brought home some stripper or worse.

We drank lots of bourbon and water. My father grilled hamburgers in the backyard, and he was so excited and tipsy he forgot to put the meat in his bun. He was eating a huge sandwich of tomato, lettuce, onion, pickles, cheese—but no meat. We all had a big laugh.

We settled on August 18. Loretta had gone for a while to a little Methodist church out near Birmingham-Southern and Legion Field, Denman United Methodist Church. We visited a Reverend

Godby there, and he counseled us and agreed to marry us. My folks were there, Loretta's folks, her sister and her husband, and their three children with cousin Sheila. Loretta's friend Nancy Schaffer also came. Jesse and Shirley Jackson were our witnesses. Reuben Triplett stood up with me. The ceremony was simple, short, and sweet, and we were married.

We moved into a larger apartment in the basement of the building where I'd been living. I had a deal with the landlord that I would get a discount on the rent if I stoked the furnace. We had a tiny kitchen, but that was no real drawback since Loretta could cook nothing but tuna casserole. It was excellent tuna casserole, and we had it a lot. I did a lot of chili and bacon and eggs. I cooked steaks and hamburgers.

We took sunset walks around the lovely campus. One night, the weekend before classes were to begin on Monday, Loretta sprained her ankle. I had to carry her books for her when she walked on a crutch to class. One class was a large one in Comer Auditorium. There must have been seventy-five or eighty students in there as we came limping down the aisle, and every eye was on us. There was dead silence. We didn't really give a shit what anybody thought, but it was annoying just the same.

I was writing short stories. One, "The Iron Gates," was accepted by *Comment*, a magazine at the University of Alabama. It was edited at that time by Howell Raines, who was later editor in chief of *The New York Times*. Another, "The Hunted," was accepted by *The Arlington Quarterly* at the University of Dallas. The *Story* anthology of prize short stories came out and got some good reviews; my story was singled out for praise in several of them. I had been working off and on on two novels, the two I had begun in Nashville all those years ago, but I couldn't seem to get them right. I was teaching three composition courses and snowed under with papers. I was assigned to several faculty committees. I was realizing that teaching didn't provide me with as much writing time as I'd hoped, and I worked late at night and on weekends. Loretta was in demanding classes and studying hard. We didn't have time for much of a social life, other than drinking with the Jacksons and Reuben.

The Southern Literary Festival was meeting in Tuscaloosa, and I was invited to be on the program. Loretta and I were put up in the Stafford Hotel. We had drinks with John Craig Stewart and his new wife; John was writer in residence at the University of South Alabama in Mobile. Another writer on the program was Jesse Hill Ford, who had recently made a major splash with a novel called *The Liberation of Lord Byron Jones.* Jesse had written me in admiration of "The Stone Soldier," and we were pleased to meet in person. (We corresponded regularly for years after that. Our letters are among my papers at the Alabama Writers' Collection at Auburn University.) Eudora Welty was the headline writer. I met her and talked with her at a cocktail party at Professor O. B. Emerson's apartment. (The bartender at that party was a young graduate student named Norman McMillan. Norman would later come to teach at Montevallo, serve as chairman of the department, and become a lifelong friend.)

We were invited out to have tea with Hudson Strode and his wife. Mr. Strode was a legendary teacher of creative writing and Shakespeare at UA who claimed Demopolis as a hometown (not true). He was an elegantly dressed banty rooster of a man who was an inveterate name-dropper. He showed me a framed letter on the wall with a presidential seal and told me it was from "Dwight." He strutted when he walked. Dr. Strode arranged the chairs in the room so that he and the guest of honor, the well-respected fiction writer Caroline Gordon, the wife of the poet Allen Tate, were seated together with the rest of us lesser lights grouped in front of them as an audience. He proceeded to perform for us. Later, Loretta and I ran into Ms Gordon in the elevator at the hotel, and we all had a huge laugh about the afternoon.

The new editor of *Comment* magazine in Tuscaloosa was an extraordinarily gifted young poet named John Finlay. He published my story "A Very Proper Resting Place." John could be effusive. In his acceptance note, he had written "You honor *Comment* the way Lowell was said to honor the Pulitzer Prize." John looked the way poets ought to look: narrow of build, a handsome face under a thick mop of curly blond hair. He was the type that women wanted to nurture, to take care of. He was an admirer of T. S. Eliot, Ivor Winters, and Allen Tate and a devout Episcopalian. I would later stand next to him in church as we sang his favorite hymn, "A Mighty Fortress Is Our God." John bellowed in a loud and profoundly off-key voice.

Loretta did her practice teaching at Montevallo High School, just across the street from our building. One night we had the Jacksons over for drinks. At the time there was much apprehension and even fear about the looming integration of the schools, and Jesse and Shirley got loud and drunk, yelling at us about all the ills of public education and touting the coming formation of a segregation academy, a "private school" outside of town. They were so obnoxious that I ordered them out of our apartment. Shirley cried, but they left. Though we continued to be civil, we were never close friends after that.

Loretta graduated with honors and took a job teaching in a small, three-teacher school out in an old mining community, Maylene. She had no training in elementary education, but she taught third and fourth grades in the same room. She loved it. We now had two salaries, so we moved to a new place, a roomy apartment on two floors in an old building on King Street, across from the college president's home. We had a front screen porch, where we could sit and look out over the president's broad, manicured lawn as though it were ours. We had to buy some new furniture, a hide-a-bed sofa (which we still have in our living room) and a pecan dining room set.

Loretta wanted to go to graduate school at Bread Loaf School of English in Vermont, a part of Middlebury College. It is the English school of the summer language program, not to be confused with the famous Bread Loaf Writers Conference, which meets every year on the same campus at the end of the summer. (During the years we were there, we went to the writers' conference some and have been back since.) The school draws its faculty from some of the finest universities in the nation—and around the world. Loretta had courses under professors from Brown, San Francisco State, Harvard, Johns Hopkins, the University of Virginia, Smith College, Columbia University, and the University of Edinburgh in Scotland.

Mr. Davidson had taught at Bread Loaf for twenty-two straight summers and was a highly respected professor there. We went to Nashville and spent an afternoon with him at his house. Since his retirement he was growing feebler. He was enthusiastic about Loretta attending Bread Loaf and agreed to write a recommendation for her. He assured her that she would be admitted. "They love pretty little Southern girls up there," he twinkled. Mr. Davidson had a house there, and he and his wife, Theresa (an artist), would be in residence; we made plans to work together again. One of his good friends, Dulcie Scott, also had a house on the top of a mountain nearby; she had several cottages she rented to Bread Loaf students and faculty. Mr. Davidson arranged with her to rent us one. Sadly, Mr. Davidson died late that spring, before he could leave for Vermont.

Thirteen

Dulcie Scott owned a rambling wood and log house, Deacon Hill, with a porch around two sides offering breathtaking, panoramic views. On a clear day you could see the snow-capped peaks of the Adirondack Mountains all the way on the other side of Lake Champlain, a distance of at least a hundred miles. She had entertained professors, writers, and graduate students on that porch for years. She had been a friend of Robert Frost when he lived on a farm near Ripton, just down the road. Dulcie Scott was in her late sixties with flaming red hair. She used a cigarette holder, drove a cream-colored Thunderbird, drank straight gin, and took classes at Bread Loaf every summer.

We rented a tiny two-room log cabin in her backyard. It had a primitive shower, a sink, a hot plate, and a toilet. It was heated with a wood fireplace. (The nights in the mountains of Vermont in June and July can get very cold.) It had a covered stone front porch for sitting.

Before Loretta's classes began, we met the poet William Meredith, who was to be our friend for life. He was building a ski lodge up the road beyond our cabin on property he had purchased from Dulcie. William had already published several volumes of well-received poetry. He taught during the year at Connecticut College in New London and periodically at Bread Loaf in the summers. Older than we were and younger than Dulcie, William was a fit, handsome man (we would look up to see him jogging down the dirt road) with stylishly short, graying hair. He was exceptionally personable. We were friends from the very start, joining him and Dulcie on the porch for drinks in the evenings. Like Dulcie, he drank a lot of straight gin. Years later he told us that after he'd seen us around, Dulcie told him, "Oh, you'll like them, they're real agreeable lushes."

During the Bread Loaf years, I drank heavily. The late sixties and early seventies were exhilarating years to be young and alive. We lived a bohemian life every summer in those lovely woods, but it was not idyllic. The anxiety attacks still plagued me. Every now and then I would have a touch of the hives. Just the appearance of one hive would terrify me that I was about to become covered with them. Doctors prescribed Librium and Valium, but I couldn't tell that they did me any good. The best antidote for whatever was ailing me was still liquor. With a few drinks the anxiety would go away and there would be not a trace of hives.

Though I was rarely completely sober during those summers, I worked steadily on a novel about the civil rights movement. Its tentative title was *All the Wild Summer.* I finished it, but I could never get it in the shape I wanted. I was still publishing short stories, but I was beginning to think I'd never write a successful novel. I struggled with depression, and Loretta and I both realized that I had a serious problem with alcohol. Doing something about it, however, was something else again. Once, on the way home from another sodden summer in Vermont, we sat in the car in front of a drive-in restaurant near one of our favorite motels in Brewster, New York. I told Loretta I was planning to stop drinking. Her response was an honest one: But what will become of our social life? What about parties? What will people think? Couldn't I learn to drink moderately? She liked to drink and didn't want to quit herself. I certainly didn't want to stop drinking either.

The Bread Loaf summers were wonderful ones in spite of my drinking. I managed to get a lot of writing done. We made a lot of good friends, including Bill and Gee Gee Mygdal, with whom we later traveled to Europe and Mexico. We went up to Montreal and visited the World's Fair. We went back down to Manhattan to visit Donald and his wife, Dianne, and have dinner with William Meredith at his sister's apartment near Central Park. I took Paul Gray's course in the contemporary novel and discovered Pynchon, Vonnegut, and the novels of Samuel Beckett. I smoked pot. It was Woodstock nation, an exciting time to be with young people from all over America. The times they were a-changin, and we seemed to be right in the middle of them. There were crazy, wild parties with beautiful, superintelligent people.

Our last summer there, the summer Loretta would graduate, we decided to stay down the mountain in East Middlebury. We were tired of the inconveniences of having to build fires, of the lingering smell of gas from the hotplate and the little hot water heater. We rented the ground floor of an old house down on Route 125, just across the street from the Waybury Inn. We shared the house with a young interracial couple upstairs. I was submitting short stories to *The New Yorker*; I got much nicer rejection letters with a return address in Vermont.

Fourteen

Loretta was now teaching English at Helena Middle School. She was flourishing with seventh and eighth grade kids. They adored her and she loved them. She was doing all sorts of innovative workshops with free-form learning stations, and she was very successful. Channel 13 in Birmingham came down and did a television report on her methods. The public schools were being integrated and Loretta took a leadership role in helping to bring about a peaceful transition. I taught the first two black girls to come to Montevallo in my freshman English class. We did not experience the agony and violence that occurred elsewhere, though out at Helena there were several incidences of black teachers' tires being slashed.

Winston got his PhD and took a job at the University of Alabama, an hour away. He drove over to visit us. O. B. Emerson asked me to come over there and speak to his class in the American short story. Loretta went with me and we all went out to dinner. It became a regular practice for me to go over and visit Professor Emerson's class.

And Jayne and Pat came back from Nevada. They had come home once for Christmas and Loretta had met them. Now they moved back to Demopolis. Pat had completed his studies with Walter Clark. He was still writing stories, but he didn't want to continue his schooling. They moved into a small house and Pat went to work for Vanity Fair. The company had a manufacturing plant for women's lingerie in Demopolis, and my cousin Aubrey Cobb was plant manager. (Pat loved to talk about the "fuzzy gussets" in the panties they were making.) He worked as Aubrey's subordinate before they moved to Monroeville, where he became a plant manager himself, the youngest one in the corporation. They lived there until their first child—my parents' first grandchild—was born: a little girl, Cora Cobb Brasfield.

We became a devoted foursome. We loved them—and enjoyed being with them—so much that Loretta and I went back often to visit. Pat was witty and funny; Jayne was being the young married Southern belle. We all drank heavily, too much. We played "Hearts" and "B for Botticelli" all night. We went on trips to the beach, ate tons of seafood, and frolicked in the surf. Pat and I fly-fished a lot, and we'd stop at The Good Lady's on the way home. Pat's manic behavior—his tendency to misbehave—was contagious and infected the rest of us. Not to say that I was innocent. Pat and I had always been given to doing outrageous things when we were together.

One night when they were living in Monroeville, Pat and I got drunk and wandered up and down the streets, trying "to make Boo Radley come out." "Come on out, Boo!" we'd call out in front of every house we came to. And we almost killed ourselves in Pat's new Pontiac Firebird. We were in Pensacola. Jayne was pregnant with Cora, and we were coming into town across the long bridge, Pat driving ninety miles an hour. As we came off the bridge, he lost control of the car and we spun out, plowing down a sandy ditch until we came to rest on a sand dune. Jayne, Pat, and I were so drunk that, after our initial shock, we thought it was great fun, but Loretta was shaken up by it. She could not eat her dinner. She took one of Jayne's tranquilizers and went out and went to sleep in the car. She was thoroughly pissed off at all three of us.

That was the trip when Pat and I put the kite up. We claimed it was the highest a kite had ever been flown on Pensacola Beach. I kept leaving to buy more and more string. The kite got so high it was just a tiny speck in the sky. It must have been over Pensacola Bay. Jayne and Loretta watched us from their beach towels, sipping on cold beers and laughing with us. I was to use this kite-flying incident much later, when I would deliver Pat's eulogy at his memorial service.

One of Pat's short stories won a prize in Birmingham. He came up to receive it and stayed with us. It was my birthday weekend, and Loretta cooked quail and wild rice. We drank Scotch into the night. Very late, a call came. Cora had been born.

At school I was getting good evaluations on my teaching and I was happy with my job. We had new people in the department. Norman McMillan got his PhD from the University of Michigan, and he and his wife, Joan, moved to Montevallo. Another couple, Sid Vance and his wife Barbara, came from Nashville, where Sid had received his PhD from Vanderbilt. Both men became my best friends on the faculty, and remain so until this day. Loretta liked their wives. We were often together for dinner parties. Because there were lots of young, new faculty members, the social life in Montevallo was improving. There were lots of parties. We even had dances.

Mr. Davidson's admonition about promotions proved to be accurate. I was quickly promoted to the rank of assistant professor. But when it came time to be considered for associate, I was stymied. Several people who had come after me had already been promoted. John Lott urged all the other assistants to apply for the next rank, all the assistants but me. They all had their terminal degrees and I only had a master's. After several years as an assistant,

I went to see John and told him I wanted to apply for promotion to associate professor. At that time we had a dean, something of a conservative blowhard, who had pronounced that as long as he was dean, nobody would achieve any rank above assistant without a doctorate. John wrung his hands. It won't do any good, he told me, Dean Walters was stubborn. John obviously did not want me to apply, but I thought I had a right to. "If I'm turned down," I said, "I want Dean Walters to have to look me in the eye and explain why." I was teaching three upper-division courses and had regularly published short fiction since I'd been there, and that was what I'd been hired to do. "Robert Penn Warren is a full professor, and he only has a master's," I said. "You're not Robert Penn Warren," John said. "And this ain't Yale," I said. "Please don't make waves," John pleaded. I got my package together and applied. John, against his better judgment, sent it on to Dean Walters. When the promotions were announced, I'd been promoted to associate. Dean Walters never said a word to me. Later, when I was promoted to full professor, it was easier. I had published a novel by then and Dean Walters had retired.

William Meredith came to visit us for several stays. He gave a reading at the college, and I drove him over to Tuscaloosa, where he read his poetry. On another of his visits we were at a literary party that some people in Birmingham were giving for him. I had been dry for months. The host took drink orders; Loretta asked for a gin and tonic, and I told the host, "Just tonic." He brought me a strong gin and tonic *without ice*. I drank it down and was off again.

William drank as much as I did. (Most people called him "Bill" Meredith. Only his closest friends called him William.) At the conclusion of one of his visits he went with me into Birmingham, where I was to accept the first prize award in the Hackney short story competition at a crowded luncheon in the still-under-construction new civic center. I read the story and William was introduced. I took him on to the airport, and we sat in the bar and drank martinis. I poured him on the plane back to Connecticut.

I finished my novel and gave it the title *Coming of Age at the Y.* (The heroine lives at the YWCA, just as Loretta had.) Al wanted me to come to New York to talk about strategy for marketing the book, so Loretta's sister Annette came to stay with Meredith while we flew up there for several days. Donald had just published a nonfiction book called *Inner Running* and was hard at work on a novel. The Porters had Al and his wife to dinner.

Al had shown the manuscript to a couple of editors. He didn't think he could market it in New York. He wanted to find a small, regional press to bring it out. Hopefully it would get some good reviews that we could use in shopping my next one around. And there was always the possibility that some large publisher would pick it up for paperback rights. I was bitterly disappointed. I could feel my old depression creeping in. I told Al to just put it on hold.

John Finlay came and joined the faculty at Montevallo and took an apartment in the same building where Loretta and I lived. The three of us became devoted friends and remained so until John died of AIDS in 1991. John lived alone, and every evening around five he showed up at our door ready to join us for cocktails. Usually he stayed for dinner. Then later he might come back in his robe and slippers for a nightcap. Once John decided he was going to have us up for supper, to "pay us back," he said. He served canned tomato soup and beer. I looked in his refrigerator; there was nothing in there but beer and a carton of cigarettes.

John wrote poetry and read all night. We were together often until John left to go back to graduate school at LSU. John went to the island of Corfu, in Greece, where he lived for a while. He would come to Montevallo for long visits with us, even after we moved out to our house in the country and our daughter was born.

John was an amazing, remarkable poet. He published two small collections of poems and some criticism, particularly on Ivor Winters. After his early and untimely death, a group of his friends published an anthology of appreciation of his work. John was a gentle soul, given to occasional excesses of emotional outburst. He was a poor classroom teacher, in that he could not keep his rolls straight and get his papers graded. He would sometimes not show up for class for days at a time. He would invite students over to his apartment, where they would sit on the floor and he would drink Scotch and talk to them about poetry all night. At least one of those former students has since told me that she learned more from John Finlay during those sessions than in all of her other classes combined.

Ironically, John Lott called me into his office one day and asked me if I thought John had a drinking problem. I told him no, I thought John had a "living" problem. He was just too raw and sensitive for this world, and it killed him. At the end he went home to his mother's farm near Enterprise in South Alabama, where she took care of him. We visited them there. His mother was a saintly woman; in 1991 not much was known about AIDS. She stoically and courageously, with only the help of John's sister, nursed him until he died. John had converted to Roman Catholicism in his last years. His family read Psalms to him as he lay dying.

I was trying to revise *Coming of Age at the Y.* I kept a bottle in my studio in the basement, so I could go down there at night to be alone, to sit at my desk and drink while I wrote. Loretta had gotten a part-time position at the college so she'd have more time for Meredith. I'd go home in the middle of the day and have a few drinks. I taught classes under the influence; I went to church under the influence. I wrote under the influence. I thought a lot about my Uncle Russell. I still do. The last glimpse I had of him: He was puking blood into a wastebasket in the hospital, an image that is indelibly etched on my brain.

Loretta went up to Vincent to a funeral and decided to spend the night with her mother. I was in one of my dry periods, so she left Meredith at home with me. Meredith was about eight years old. I had bottles hidden all over the house, and with my policewoman gone, I thought I could have a few drinks. I got sloppy drunk and passed out on the floor. Meredith was alarmed and frightened. She called her mother, and Loretta came home. She was disgusted with me, beyond furious.

I was untruthful to Loretta. When she would ask me if I'd been drinking, I'd lie. She was the most important person in my life. I knew she was the best thing that had ever happened to me. Yet the booze was somehow important enough for me to lie to her face. I knew she loved me, but I could see that a part of her was beginning to hate me for what was happening to me. Addiction drains the soul of all hope and comfort. The alcoholic without his alcohol is in a frigid, cold, terrifying, lonely world that he knows will destroy him if he doesn't find a buffer, a drink. It makes little sense, but it is real.

Make no mistake about it: Alcoholism is a disease, as genuine a disease as diabetes or cancer. Untreated, it is chronic and fatal. It is a cunning, baffling disease that has no cure, only a treatment. I know now that I have a genetic disposition to addiction, that I was born with the gene for it. I have a chemical imbalance in my brain. So did my Uncle Russell, I have no doubt. When he came along, nobody understood it. He was thought to just have poor willpower. He, like millions of other men and women, died an early death because medical science had not yet learned the truth about alcoholism. If there is a single key to my recovery, it's that in rehab I discovered that I had a treatable *disease*, absolutely nothing to feel guilty about. I was not cured; I was treated. I was an alcoholic when I was born, and I'll be an alcoholic when I die.

I was teaching in summer session, but I was having a difficult time. I was drinking heavily. It was becoming increasingly harder for Loretta to have much patience with me. She was seeing Judy Prince, a therapist we had both seen for years, a lot for help. I went on a binge. For years I had sometimes had a drink in the morning, a Bloody Mary or a hair-of-the-dog snort, to get me going, to ward off the shakes and the demons. Now I was doing it every day. I would drink until I felt the "click," that point when I felt "normal," when the horrors of incipient delirium tremens receded to the shadows of my mind and I could get on with my day. I had to have nips all day to keep my buzz going. Long gone were the days when I was a good ol' boy hell-raiser. I was a pluperfect, certified drunk.

I began to miss classes. (I had missed them before. There were Mondays when I had a "stomach virus.") One day I came home and Loretta was gone. She had taken Meredith and gone to her mother's house. My first response was, "Good, now I can drink all I want to and there'll be nobody to nag me." Loretta called that night. She said she couldn't do it anymore. She loved me, but she couldn't stand to stay in that situation any longer. She said she hadn't left me. But she wasn't coming home until I did something about my drinking.

Fifteen

I was at Jim Rogers's townhouse, on Riverside Drive in Manhattan. It was a party for the release of the paperback edition of my novel *A Walk Through Fire*, which William Morrow and Company had published the previous year. It was an elegant cocktail affair, with a bartender and a uniformed butler passing drinks. Jim, a very generous and gracious man whom I had known when we were boys in Demopolis, hosted the party for me. It was a bright, sparkling autumn afternoon, the sun brushing the leaves in Riverside Park across the street and glinting on the Hudson River just beyond.

Susan Leon, my editor at Morrow, was there. Other guests were Al Zuckerman, my literary agent, and his wife, Eileen Gouge, a novelist; Howell Raines, executive editor of *The New York Times*, who'd published one of my short stories years ago when he was editor of the magazine *Comment*; Donald Porter and his wife, Dianne; the novelist Cassandra King; and of course, Loretta.

Jim Rogers had invited me to stay at his townhouse several years before, when I had a play in rehearsal in New York, and we had become friends. He had retired, at age thirty-seven, from the Quantum Fund, a hedge fund he'd managed with George Soros, taking with him a profit of some $40 million At that time he was a bachelor who lived the high life, a man who had all of Manhattan as his playground. He dated beautiful, glamorous women, dined in all the nicest restaurants, and drank the finest wines.

I did not join him with the wines, and I asked the bartender only for club soda. I was finally sober and had been so for about six years. Those six years had been positive, energetic, and productive. I still suffered from depression. I took an antidepressant and saw a therapist periodically. But I was not drinking. For the first time in my life, for almost as long as I could remember, I had no alcohol in my blood, full or half life, or in my liver.

After I had gotten out of rehab, at the end of the summer in 1984, shaky but with a kind of fragile confidence and determination, I did a final rewrite and revision of *Coming of Age at the Y.* I called Al Zuckerman and told him to go ahead and find a small publisher for it. Portals Press of Tuscaloosa and New Orleans accepted the novel. Portals was run by James Travis, who was a retired professor of classics at Columbia University in New York, and his son, John, who managed the New Orleans branch of the company. I drove over to Tuscaloosa and met him; he was elderly and eccentric but enthusiastic about my book.

I decided to go to St. Luke's Church in Mountain Brook for AA. I didn't want to go. I had had to agree to go to three meetings a week before I left rehab, and I violated that pledge the very first week I was out. I didn't, and still don't, like to "join" things. Groups made me nervous. I knew that dealing with my anxiety and depression was going to be as difficult as abstaining from drinking.

About fifteen or twenty years before, I had come clean and told our old family physician, Leslie Hubbard, about my fears of being an alcoholic. He was a wonderful doctor, but of the old school.

He told me if I suspected it, I was probably right, and I should stop drinking. He said he had several patients who went to AA. A couple of nights later, the phone rang, and it was some man inviting me to go with him to a meeting. He sounded about a hundred years old. I was polite, but I told him no thanks. I had gone right back to the booze.

It was an hour's drive up to St. Luke's, an hour back. But I didn't want to go to a meeting in Montevallo. I think what I feared most was running into someone I knew, who would welcome me and want to talk about my problem, maybe some jerk on the faculty who would immediately assume we could be friends. I was embarrassed about being an alcoholic. I didn't want to talk about it with anybody. I was not drinking, and a part of me wanted to believe that that was enough; the better part—and all I'd learned in rehab—was telling me to be careful that I wasn't turning into a dry drunk. I was still moody and quick to anger. I constantly reminded myself of the HALT admonition that I had learned at the lodge. Be careful if you are: Hungry, Angry, Lonely, or Tired.

It was during those times that you were likely to BUD, build up to drink. I "budded" all the time. When I found myself "budding," I would immediately have to say HALT! Often out loud, which elicited some puzzled looks if I was around other people.

The St. Luke's setup was perfect for us, as it was large enough that they had an Alanon and an Alateen meeting at the same time as my meeting. Even though Meredith was only eleven, she was mature beyond her years and Loretta and I felt that she could benefit from being with other children of alcoholics. And we were Episcopalians; we knew the church, it was familiar to us. I felt awkward and anxious going to my first meeting. I didn't want to have to get up and talk in front of people. I didn't want to say, "Hi, I'm Bill, I'm an alcoholic." It seemed to me forced and artificial. I thought I'd feel silly saying it.

I managed to make it through that first meeting okay. The alcoholics met first all together in one large group, then split up into discussion groups. I picked the one on the Twelve Steps, the series of actions and thinking that can lead one to sobriety; it is the recovering alcoholic's mantra. A middle-aged man named Steve conducted the discussion. We were to go around the room and tell what step we each were on, and we'd talk about it. My first thought was, "Oh shit, I knew it!" If I wasn't going to speak, I would have to *say* I wasn't going to, and maybe have to give a reason. I started to childishly imagine that I'd been tricked, and it pissed me off. When it got to me, I said I hadn't started on them yet.

"Oh yes, you have," Steve said, smiling, "you're here." He pointed to a poster with the Twelve Steps listed. The first step is "Admitted to yourself that you are powerless over alcohol." I explained that I hadn't "formally" begun the "systematic" working through the steps. I sounded to myself like some academic prick. Everybody just looked at me. No one laughed at me, at least out loud. I felt better, but I was far from totally won over.

Alcoholics Anonymous is a remarkable institution. There are chapters of it all over the world. Everywhere you go, there are meetings. I was recently on a cruise ship on the Mediterranean, and I saw listed on one day's activities "Friends of Bill." (Bill W. was the founder of AA, back in the late thirties.) I have looked up AA in the phone books in Rome, Paris, London, Athens, Galway, and they are there. There are no membership rolls, no dues (only contributions). It is run entirely by its members, who are all recovering alcoholics. There is a central office that oversees the publications and organizes periodic large gatherings in different parts of the country. But there is no president, no CEO. It is probably the most truly democratic society in the world. Countless men and women owe their very lives to it, and lifetime members are fiercely loyal.

The three of us went faithfully to meetings every Tuesday night for the next two years. We made a family outing out of it. We would go in early, go to the Galleria Mall, and eat in the food court. Meredith could do some browsing and shopping. (Loretta hates shopping as much as I do, so we split up the task of taking her around.) We'd go to our meetings and then drive home, arriving a little after ten o'clock, which was late for Meredith on a school night, but she didn't complain. The meetings were still tedious for me. I heard the same stories, from the same people, over and over again. I realized that they needed to tell their stories, and I needed to be there and listen to them, for me as well as them. But some nights it was like listening to fingernails on a blackboard or being forced to look at Norman Rockwell paintings for an hour. Their stories were sentimental and maudlin, sometimes full of observations that made me want to say, "You have a firm grasp of the obvious."

Loretta and I also began attending Continuing Care at Brookwood Hospital every Thursday night. I liked that better because it was a controlled environment directed by counselors. There were three therapy groups: one for the patients, one for the spouses, and one large one for both, presided over by Marion Cranford. For the first year Loretta and I went to the separate groups. Then we graduated into the larger group. Marion was a terrific counselor, and she had to be, as there were arguments and fights, insults and weeping. Sometimes there were relapses and people would show up drunk.

After two years, they had a banquet for us out at the lodge. They gave us each a medal. I didn't see a single one of the men who'd been in treatment with me. We listened to a long testimonial from some guy, one that I would have sworn I had heard before, word for word. I had not had a relapse. I had become one of those who stood an eighty percent chance of recovering.

My first novel was published in November 1985, a little over a year after I was released from rehab. (I once read that publishing a first novel or a book of poems was like dropping a pebble off the Brooklyn Bridge and listening for a splash. That would be especially true of a first novel from a small, regional press.) Portals did not have a decent distribution and the book was not widely reviewed, though most of the notices it got were positive. One reviewer called the bawdy, ribald novel "a comic masterpiece." But another said it "made him ashamed to be a Southerner." In the coming few years I gave readings from *Coming of Age at the Y* on many college campuses around the Southeast and the novel acquired quite a following, becoming something of an underground favorite. It sold moderately well and continues to in a trade paperback.

I was feeling good and energetic. I set to work on *The Hermit King*, a novel I'd worked on off and on since the first Nashville years, about the old black man Joe Bynymo. Al Zuckerman felt that it was not commercial enough for the New York market. I finished it, and, again, Jim Travis at Portals accepted it with enthusiasm. I began to write plays. I took the last chapter of a failed novel I had based loosely on Loretta's life and began molding it into a full-length play. Writing for the stage proved to be more difficult than I had imagined, but I continued working on it. Al, meanwhile, was pestering me to write something more salable, my "breakthrough" novel, as he called it. I was fishing around for a subject that inspired me.

I heard of the Atlantic Center for the Arts, and I was interested. It was in New Smyrna Beach, on the east coast of Florida. I ordered a brochure; one component of the summer workshop was literary. Each session had three well-known, accomplished artists: a writer, a visual artist, and a musician. Each artist accepted ten associates to work with for six weeks. The writer for the next summer was Romulus Linney, a playwright I greatly admired. (I had seen a local production of his *Holy Ghosts* in Birmingham.) I didn't have any finished plays to submit with my application so I sent fiction. (Linney was also a novelist.) I was accepted.

Loretta, Meredith, and I lived for the six weeks in a small cottage on the beach. It was actually part of an old, vintage 1950s-era motel owned by a retired commercial fisherman we called the

"Old Salt." The nine other people in the workshop were from all over the country, most of them with produced plays. One was from New York with off-Broadway credits and one was a playwright in residence at the Denver Center Theater Company. Beverly Trader, a highly successful writer of children's plays, was from Atlanta. Ann Deagon, a poet originally from Birmingham whom I knew slightly, lived in another of the Old Salt's cottages. We met every day, all day, with Linney, a lean, middle-aged Southerner, who led the discussions. We read and acted our own scenes and portions of his plays. Romulus was an exceptional teacher, guiding me to a deeper understanding of the stage and of my own play.

Naturally, with that many artistic people gathered together, there were parties and a good bit of drinking (and dope smoking as well). So my newfound sobriety was tested several times. All the associates were intelligent and attractive. I forged a friendship with Beverly Trader, and later Loretta and I would visit her and her husband in Atlanta. Beverly and I went to numerous plays together over the next decade.

Loretta had always wanted to travel more, but I had been resistant. When I was drinking, I was worried that I'd lose control, or get cut off from my source of liquor. Now that I was making progress with my sobriety, we took Meredith on a trip to London, my first foray to Europe. I continued to be amazed at the sectors of experience that were opened up to me since I wasn't drinking. I had known my active addiction was restricting me, but I had not *known* it. We stayed in an old hotel near Kensington Gardens that was right out of Dickens. Meredith and Loretta went out to Bath and then to Canterbury. I stayed in London and went to plays. I saw eight new plays in seven days. The exchange rate at that time was so good that tickets to the plays cost half as much as they would have in New York. All of us went to see *Noises Off.* I saw a new Pinter play and discovered Sam Shepherd, a fantastic American playwright I had to go all the way to London to find. I was blown away by a production of *Fool for Love* and I wondered what those nicely dressed, sophisticated Londoners thought of the picture of Barbara Mandrell the old man points to at the end of the play.

I became more involved in campus politics. I had always belonged to AAUP, the American Association of University Professors, but now I grew more active. I had once before been elected to the faculty senate. I was again elected and served one year as its president. I was now a senior professor, and my legendary consumption of beverages seemed not something that had permanently damaged my reputation. I went to parties and receptions with Loretta. She, when she went to the bar for her own drink, would bring me a club soda or an ice water. I was self-conscious at first, but few people seemed to notice that I wasn't drinking. I was becoming more comfortable with my new, abstemious self. I had little trouble ignoring the liquor cabinet at home; when friends came over, I had club soda or an O'Doul's. But sometimes I could almost taste Scotch on my tongue, and I had to will myself away from it. On hot days I thought about cold beers. O'Doul's didn't really cut it; I eventually discovered Kaliber, an imported nonalcoholic beer made by Guinness, expensive but much better.

We were invited up to Athens State College, in the northern part of the state, for a conference featuring the playwright and screenwriter Horton Foote. There was a showing of his film *Tomorrow*, lectures, discussions, and book signings. Jackson Fentry in *Tomorrow* was Robert Duvall's first leading role; Duvall had famously debuted as Boo Radley in *To Kill a Mockingbird*, for which Foote had won his first Academy Award for writing the screenplay. An old friend and colleague of ours, James Chasteen, was then president of Athens State. He and his wife invited us to stay with them in the president's home. They had a reception for Mr. Foote. During the course of the evening the two of us became friends. He and I were the only two people not drinking—we discovered we were both in the AA fraternity—and we wound up the evening with him playing the piano and me joining him in singing old hymns. He knew Romulus Linney in New York. He agreed to read my play, which I had finished and entitled *Sunday's Child*.

One night he called me and told me he thought it was a very good play. He suggested I send it to Marlene Mancini, a director at HB Playwrights Foundation in New York. The "HB" was Herbert Berghoff, an eminent director who had directed the first American production of Beckett's *Waiting for Godot*, and who was married to Uta Hagan, one of the finest American actors of the twentieth century. The Foundation was connected to the HB Studio, an acting school in Greenwich Village, and was dedicated to bringing noncommercial plays to New York, plays that might not otherwise be seen. The plays were done at a small studio theater on Bank Street. Both Romulus Linney and Horton Foote had had plays mounted there, the first production of *Tomorrow* with Robert Duvall being one of them. The actors were mostly equity, some who taught at the HB Studio and others who were working actors around the city. The Foundation had a contract exemption with Actors' Equity which allowed these people to work there without being paid scale.

It was months before I heard from Ms. Mancini. When she called, she told me they wanted to do *Sunday's Child*; the holdup had been that they'd been waiting on Celeste Holm, an Academy Award–winning actress, to accept the leading role. Ms. Holm had agreed to do it and was sitting in her office right that minute. Ms. Holm got on the phone and told me she loved my play and was looking forward to playing the part of Martha. Ms. Mancini got back on and asked me if I could come to New York to sign the contract and attend a read-through with the actors.

Sixteen

I was thrilled at the prospect of my play being produced—with an actor as famous as Celeste Holm!—but I was apprehensive about going to New York—and into the theater world—so soon after rehab. I knew it would be another test, this one a major one. I called my counselor, Marion Cranford, who assured me she thought I could do it. In the next couple of days I had four phone calls from men in Manhattan, giving me their numbers and inviting me to go with them to their AA groups.

I didn't go to any meetings in Manhattan. But I derived a great deal of strength and resolve from the fact that I had so many people in my corner. I felt a part of something larger than myself, a connection with the bigger world. Ironically, the fact that I *didn't* go to meetings didn't keep AA from being a source of stability and fortitude for me.

Marlene Mancini met me at LaGuardia Airport. She was a robust, attractive young woman of Italian descent who spoke with a heavy New York accent. She drove me, in her tiny car, weaving in and out of heavy traffic, into Manhattan to the theater, where I met Celeste Holm and some of the other actors. Ms. Holm's husband, the Shakespearean actor Wesley Addy, was also in the play, in the role loosely based on Loretta's father. We all adjourned to a little bar called The Sazerac, around the corner on Hudson Street, for drinks. Marlene drank straight vodka; I stuck with club soda. Marlene and I both ordered a bowl of soup. The others sat with us around a long table, in what was to be a familiar circumstance during my stays in New York with my plays, with the actors and the technical people going out after rehearsals for drinks. The Sazerac was dim and comfortable, the talk stimulating and exciting to me. The actors praised my play and seemed to have a great deal of respect for it.

Then Marlene drove me uptown to Donald and Dianne's apartment, where I was staying. The Porters had sold the loft building and moved up to West 71st Street, just off Central Park. Donald had recently published his first novel, *Jubilee Jim and the Wizard of Wall Street*, with Putnam. They had adopted two little girls and moved away from the more bohemian neighborhood of Soho. Don, Dianne and I, the next evening, walked all over Midtown, Don and I excited with our respective successes. I stayed two more days and watched a read-through and an early rehearsal.

Marlene and Herbert Berghoff wanted me there to help in developing the play. I went home to make arrangements to return to New York for a longer period. Donald and I had looked at apartments in the paper, and everything we could find was prohibitively expensive. I didn't know where I would stay, so Donald suggested I call Jim Rogers, from Demopolis. Jim was younger than us, but we both knew him, both from our hometown and as a TV Wall Street personality. He had a regular show on CNBC and made frequent appearances on the network news and morning shows. Jim had gone to Yale and to Oxford as a Rhodes Scholar; he lived alone in a five-story townhouse on Riverside Drive.

Jim was very generous. He said to come on up, he would give me use of the fourth floor, I could come and go as I pleased, and his housekeeper, Anna, would take care of me. I moved into a front bedroom overlooking the Drive and Riverside Park, and beyond that the Hudson River. The townhouse was on 106th and Riverside, near Columbia University and the Cathedral of St. John the Divine, a 45-minute subway ride from Greenwich Village, where the HB Studio Theater was located.

I was extremely fortunate to have such luxury, so much room, in Manhattan. There was a deck on the roof, with a sauna and a hot tub. I had free run of the house. Jim was often out of town, even out of the country, and I lived there alone. Loretta flew up about a week and a half before opening night. She would go to rehearsals with me every night, and after rehearsal we would sometimes ride back uptown with Celeste and Wes in their car. They lived in a fabulous apartment on Central Park West, near The Dakota. Another prominent actor in *Sunday's Child* was Rochelle Oliver, who had starred in several of Horton Foote's movies. We also got to be good friends, and she later provided Loretta and me comps to see her in *Driving Miss Daisy* on Broadway.

Meredith flew up with Jayne and Olga Porter for opening night. It was SRO. Horton, out of loyalty to me, had come to some rehearsals and given us notes. I would see him strolling up Hudson Street, a stunningly handsome man with his overcoat thrown over his shoulders like a cape; on second look I realized it really *was* a cape, a fashion statement unremarked in Greenwich Village. Horton was there opening night with his daughters Hallie, an actor, and Daisy, a playwright. Hallie Foote had starred, with Rochelle, in a trilogy of films called *The Orphans' Home Cycle*, written by her father. The actor Fritz Weaver, who is now married to Rochelle, was there to see her in the part. Also in the audience was Uta Hagan.

Sunday's Child had a limited run of three weeks. Every night it played to full houses. A group of my friends from Montevallo and colleagues from the university came up to see it. The Main Street Players, the local community theater, had done a workshop production of the play, and many of the Montevallo actors were there. Everybody afterward went to a little Italian restaurant, Finalmente, where the Montevallo actors got to visit with their New York counterparts. Robert Friedman, a drama agent, saw the production and asked me if he could represent it and any other plays I wrote. Al Zuckerman saw it and pronounced it "small time, like the plays of Horton Foote." He was trying to get me to start thinking in terms of making big money. Horton, of course, had just won his second Academy Award for Best Screenplay for *Tender Mercies*. Al was not too happy that I'd signed with Bob Friedman; he had read some of the tentative beginnings of my new novel about the Civil Rights Movement, and he wanted me to forget plays and "get on with it."

I *was* making some progress on the novel. I got out my old manuscript of *All the Wild Summer*, which I had worked on during the Bread Loaf years. I junked most of it, but used it as the genesis for the new one, to be set in Hammond, a small Southern town, in 1961, the year of the Freedom Riders. (I had called Demopolis "Hammond" as far back as "The Stone Soldier" and in *The Hermit King*; I continued to use that as the name of my town.) But I also completed a new play, a long one-act, *Early Rains*, which Friedman promptly showed to Marlene Mancini. She called to say she liked it, but there might be some difficulty with the casting. It was basically a three-character play: two adolescent girls and a homeless old man, a street person. She would have to cast students at the Studio in the lead roles, and she didn't know if they had two that age who were up to it. She got the fantastic British character actor Michael Higgins interested in playing the old man, so she went ahead and cast two young girls in the roles. She set the opening for the next spring.

The Hermit King was published. Because I'd had a play produced in New York with another one on the way and had published two novels, Montevallo made me writer in residence. I had a reduced teaching load and plenty of time now to write. Al was enthusiastic about what I'd done on the novel. He thought I was writing a "blockbuster." He told me and Loretta over lunch at a Korean restaurant that we would soon be rich, that our lives would be forever changed. I was not sure I wanted to write a "blockbuster," but I would take whatever came. He seemed baffled that Loretta and I were not overjoyed at his prediction.

When rehearsals began for *Early Rains*, there was an immediate controversy. The script called for the two young girls, teenagers, to play the first half of the drama in panties and bras, a detail that I thought emphasized their innocence and vulnerability. Marlene wanted them in bodysuits, and Herbert Berghoff disagreed, insisting they had to be in their underwear. "You cut the balls off his play," Herbert shouted in his heavy accent. Both Marlene and Loretta were convinced that Herbert and I were simply two dirty old men who wanted to see the very attractive young actresses in their underwear. In the end, Marlene prevailed. In the theater, it is the director who is the final word, nobody else. Not the producer, not the playwright. So they played in bodysuits, which to this day I believe was a mistake, but that's ancient history now.

People came from all over New York to see Michael Higgins in my play. Norman and Joan McMillan flew up again. Loretta, Meredith, and one of her little friends stayed with me a week at Jim Rogers's place. They did all the touristy things, saw all the sights. They went to Central Park with Don and Dianne and their girls for a picnic on Mother's Day. I was working. I would go home after a performance with suggestions for improvement, work on the revisions all day, and give the new pages to the actors that night at the theater. They would do the new lines without missing a syllable. I continued to be amazed at how dedicated and hardworking New York actors are. I believe they are among the most disciplined artists in the world. Most of them, even those who had established a respected place in the theater, were still studying their craft. I had one actor who did my play each night, was in a soap opera that was taped live at a studio in Midtown at noon five days a week, and was rehearsing a new play in the afternoons. I still marvel at how they did it.

Most nights after rehearsals we went to a bar across the street from the theater. Michael Higgins drank prodigious amounts of whiskey and gin and held forth for the rest of us, gathered around a large table. He told us theater stories and tales from his days at The Old Vic Theater in London. As the evening would draw to a close, everybody would toss various amounts of money onto the table, and there was always enough to pay for the drinks and provide an adequate tip. Though there were times when I was sorely tempted to join them, I held fast and stuck to club soda. I have imbibed enough club soda over the years to float ten battleships.

When I got home after the run of *Early Rains*, my ophthalmologist told me that the cataract in my right eye was now "ripe" for surgery. Some years before I had had surgery on my left eye and had a plastic lens implant. At that time I had had to go in the hospital for several days. This time it would be outpatient, done with a laser. I had the surgery done and my vision improved immensely. I now had lens implants in *both* my eyes. I was becoming a bionic man. Little did I suspect that I would one day become even more bionic and have a shunt in my brain and plastic tubes running down to my abdomen as the result of a debilitating condition that I would develop.

I continued working on the new novel and finished a new play, *A Place of Springs*, which Marlene wanted to do at HB Studio Theater as a vehicle for Amy Wright, who had been nominated for a Tony for her role in Lanford Wilson's *The Fifth of July* and had been in the movies *The Deer Hunter* and *Stardust Memories*. She had also starred as Sabbath Lily in John Houston's film of Flannery O'Connor's novel *Wise Blood*. Marlene scheduled the play for the following summer. Meanwhile, Alliance Theater Company in Atlanta was interested in doing *Sunday's Child*. Celeste Holm was adamant that she wanted to go with the play, insisting that she had originated the role of Martha, and she put pressure on Robert

Friedman and on me. But Alliance had their own actress for the role, Mary Nell Santa Croce, a wonderful actor who had also been in *Wise Blood*, and whom Loretta and I had seen in the Alliance Theater production of Arthol Fugard's *The Road to Mecca*. Negotiations fell through.

A Place of Springs opened in New York on June 27, 1989, starring Amy Wright, with Gary Cookson, Julie Follansbee, and Sam Stonebrunner in supporting roles. It was directed by Marlene Mancini. As rehearsals progressed, Amy, Gary, and I would often go for long walks afterward, have dinner someplace, and usually wind up at Amy's apartment on Washington Square. Gary and I would share a cab back uptown. During the run of the play Meredith babysat some with Amy's little girl, Katy, who was the daughter of actor Rip Torn. Again, the play had SRO audiences.

One interesting sidelight that summer was that the death of Geraldine Page, one of America's preeminent actors, occurred during the play's run. This created quite a buzz around the theater, because Rip Torn was still married to her; they no longer lived together, but they had been married for many years. Amy, of course, was seeing Rip Torn and they had a child together. The burning question was whether or not Amy should attend the memorial. It was all just idle talk, because I knew that Amy had never intended to go, though she knew, loved, and respected Geraldine Page.

After the first of the year, I completed the manuscript of the new novel, which I had called *Look Away, Look Away*, after an old novel by James Street that I had admired when I was a teenager. The line, of course, comes from the Civil War song "Dixie." Al didn't like the title; he felt it was too negative. Al's wife, the novelist Eileen Goudge (she and Loretta had become shopping buddies), observed that the novel had numerous references to fire and suggested I find something with fire in it. I settled on a passage from the forty-third chapter of Isaiah: "When you pass through the waters I will be with you; and through the rivers, they shall not overwhelm you; when you walk through fire you shall not be burned, and the flame shall not consume you." I decided on the title *A Walk Through Fire*. Al began to shop the novel around.

William Morrow and Company made an offer, a six-figure advance that was more money than I ever thought I'd see at one time. In addition, Avon Books, a division of Morrow, wanted to purchase the mass market paperback rights, which added another substantial sum. I worked with Susan Leon, a senior editor, who told me that Morrow wanted to make the novel their lead fiction for the fall list. The first thing Susan asked me to do was cut 100 pages from the 500-page manuscript, which I thought surely would cut the balls off the novel, to borrow a phrase from Herbert Berghof. But I was wrong; I worked diligently to delete a subplot involving a character who became a minor figure and the novel was greatly improved. Susan Leon was let go in the middle of the editing process, and I went to New York to meet my new editor, who was not enthusiastic about the novel. I was confused and disappointed, but naive. I didn't know what was going on. Morrow had decided not to promote the novel, had dropped their plan to put it at the top of their fall list, but they didn't inform me. I had no idea what a terrible thing they were doing to me. Morrow effectively stymied my career, and they did not care. They gave me a huge advance and then let the book die, so that after that, for the rest of my writing life, editors and agents would simply type in my name on their computers and look at my sales record and see that it did not "sell through," that is, it did not earn back the advance against royalties. Of course, there was no asterisk to say that it was through no fault of mine. *A Walk Through Fire* is a fine novel of which I am proud and my pride is in no way diminished by the way it was treated by William Morrow and Company.

Seventeen

A *Walk Through Fire* was published on September 1, 1991. It carried enthusiastic blurbs from Horton Foote, Eileen Goudge, Jesse Hill Ford, Andrew Hudgens, and Richard Yates, whom I had recently gotten to know when he was a visiting writer in Tuscaloosa. When the reviews came in, they were all good, but Morrow did not push the major review venues for space. Al had recently taken on the British best-selling writer Ken Follett at Writers House and finally had himself a blockbuster novelist, so he had little time for me; many of my phone calls to him were not returned. Morrow did not arrange many signings. I went to the Southeastern Booksellers Association convention at the Opryland Hotel in Nashville, where I met Rosemary Danielle, who also had a Morrow novel that year, *The Hurricane Season*. Her novel got the same treatment, or lack of, as mine. Ours was a friendship that grew and flowered in the coming years. Rosemary—charming, beautiful, and outrageous—is still a good friend. Later, Pat Conroy and I would be the only two men to address her Zona Rosa women's writing conference. She said we "were men with the souls of women."

Morrow sent me to the Southern Festival of Books, also in Nashville, where I appeared on a panel with my old friend Lee Smith, whose new novel, *The Devil's Dream*, had just been released. *A Walk Through Fire* did not sell very well (there was no advertising budget at all), and I made only a few radio and television appearances. It was not until the Avon paperback was released and I went to New York for the kickoff party at Jim Rogers's townhouse that I found out what had happened. Susan explained to me how the publishing industry works. Every season a house publishes, say, seven or eight new novels. Eight or nine months before the publication dates, all the sales representatives from around the country come to New York, where the editors of the various novels appear before them and "sell" them on their books. Since they can't go into a bookstore and recommend that the owner buy *all* of Morrow's new titles, they pick those books they think they can present to them successfully and that will then sell well. The books within a house compete *against* each other to win that favor. Since Susan was let go, my book did not have a strong advocate before the sales reps and got lost in the shuffle.

Before I went on a promotional trip for the paperback, I had to have emergency surgery for a ruptured appendix. One day I began to notice a pain in my abdomen that got worse and worse. I called my local physician and couldn't get an appointment for a week. I kept thinking the pain would go away. I marched in an academic procession with the pain, went to a college baseball game with it. And then the pain *did* go away and I felt fine. After a couple of days the pain came back. It was much more severe and I insisted the doctor see me; he sent me directly to the emergency room at Shelby Medical Center, where I had surgery the next morning. The doctors told me my appendix ruptured when the pain went away. I was lucky that I didn't get peritonitis, and I would have if my body hadn't formed a cyst around the ruptured organ, preventing the poison from spreading all over my body. The cyst was the size of a softball, and I had a huge incision that took quite some time to heal.

Loretta and I left on my East Coast trip before I was fully healed, and Loretta had to carry the bags, as I couldn't lift. We flew to New York, then went down to Washington on the train, where I was given a party in Georgetown. Loretta and I visited William Meredith and his partner, Richard Harteis, who lived in Bethesda, Maryland. William was Librarian of Congress, the position that is now called Poet Laureate. I gave a reading at the Bethesda Center for Writers and the distributor had sent a novel entitled *The Fire Eaters*, by another William Cobb. Later, I called him. He was teaching at North Texas State, and the same thing had happened to him. He agreed to begin calling himself William *J.* Cobb, since I'd been publishing over the name the longest. He has since become the director of the writing program at Penn State University. We both decided that, henceforth, when anybody brought the other's book to one of us, we'd simply sign it. I wonder how many of those are out there.

A Walk Through Fire garnered some interest from the movie people in Hollywood. Producer Arthur Hiller, among whose credits was the incredibly successful *Love Story*, offered $10,000 for an option on the book. (An option means the buyer gets exclusive rights to the book for a set period—in this case ten months—during which he can decide if he wants to purchase the novel outright and make the film.) Al doubled the amount in a counteroffer; he felt that Hiller would take it if he was serious about the project. Hiller declined. Then Robert Duvall's company contacted Al; Duvall liked the novel and was interested in playing the part of O. B. Brewster. I told Al not to fuck this one up. If Robert Duvall wanted it, he should *give* it to him. After several months, they, too, declined; they were concerned that all the recent movies about the Civil Rights Movement (*Mississippi Burning*, *The Long Walk Home*, etc.) had been money losers, and as a smaller production company, they didn't want to take the chance. Horton had told me that if I sold the book, I should write the screenplay myself. When I told him I didn't know anything about writing screenplays, he offered to help me, so I was ready to go.

One day Madison Jones (*A Cry of Absence*, *An Exile)*, the writer in residence at Auburn University, called to tell me he was retiring and suggested I should apply for his position. I was tempted. But Loretta's career at Montevallo was taking off; she had moved over to the English Department, had recently founded the Harbert Writing Center, and was its first director. And Meredith was head cheerleader at Montevallo High School and was Homecoming Queen; she rebelled at the idea of leaving all her friends. So I decided to stay at Montevallo. I had essentially the same appointment that Madison did, and we loved our old house in the woods, where we had just put in a pool, our only indulgence with the advance money for *A Walk Through Fire*.

Our old friend—and my former student—Sandra King Ray moved back to Montevallo. She enrolled in the master's degree program in English and went to work as Loretta's assistant in the writing lab. The two women had lived near each other in the dorm when they were in school. They remained close friends. With me as director, Sandra wrote as her thesis a novel entitled *Making Waves in Zion*, which was very good. When she got her degree, she continued to work for Loretta and to write. She went to New York with us to meet Al Zuckerman, and he took her on as a client. Though he shopped her novel around for over a year, he was unable to find a publisher for it.

I was working on a new novel I called *Harry Reunited*. Al Zuckerman did not like it from the start. He felt I was wasting my time (and his) writing noncommercial novels that wouldn't make any money. But I was writing what I wanted and needed to write, straight from my guts. And I was certainly not satisfied with the way I'd been treated by Morrow, in spite of the big bucks. Money was not, and never had been, a motivating factor for me; I had a good job, and Meredith, Loretta, and I had all we needed. I found it unnerving when money intruded on my creative process. Al did not seem to understand this. Writers House was growing. It now occupied a townhouse in the Chelsea district and claimed other big-name clients beside Follett. Donald had already left the agency. Al had less and less time for the likes of us.

When I finished *Harry Reunited*, I was without an agent. I had heard of a new, regional publisher in Montgomery, Black Belt Press. They published Southern fiction and were acquiring a good reputation, so I called the editor in chief, Randall Williams. He was an admirer of *A Walk Through Fire* and immediately told me he was interested in publishing my new novel. I took him the manuscript. We had lunch with Wayne Greenhaw, a writer who was a partner with Randall in the press. (Both men became my good friends.) Randall accepted the novel and made plans to publish it. I suggested he read Sandra's novel. He loved it and decided to publish it, too. It was later released by Hyperion, after Sandra had made a big splash with her first novel with them, *The Sunday Wife*.

I was asked to speak and sign books at the Southern Voices Conference at the Hoover Public Library. It was there that I met two writers who became my friends, Ann Padgett and Clifton Tolbert. At the next year's conference the headline writer was Pat Conroy. I first met him at a party at library director Linda Andrews's house. Loretta and Sandra had come into town with me and were attending a party for a friend who was being made partner in her law firm, and afterward they stopped by Linda's party. Sandra was a great admirer of Pat's work. I introduced them and she blurted out, "Oh my God!" Pat was charmed. He put his arm around her shoulders and asked her if she was a writer. Not really, she replied, but she did have a novel coming out. He offered right then and there to give her a blurb, which he did.

When the novels were published, Randall sent us both to Nashville to the Southern Festival of Books, where we read from them to enthusiastic audiences. Jake Reiss, the owner of a bookstore in Birmingham, contacted Randall. Jake has now become widely known as an expert on rare and out-of-print books who also hosts signings with all the major writers in the country at his store. At that time his shop was on Highland Avenue and was known as the Highland Booksmith. He wanted to start a series of writer's appearances, particularly Alabama writers, and he wanted Sandra and me to have an event at his store. He had already had one signing, the local writer Don Keith, and he wanted to make a big impression with us. He advertised and sent out notices. It was a successful venture. Jake has since moved over the mountain to Homewood and expanded his store; it is now the Alabama Booksmith. Every writer who does the Southeast circuit wants to sign at the Alabama Booksmith.

I was also invited to appear at the Birmingham-Southern College Writing Today conference, which kicked off a fruitful relationship with them for the next decade. I was on a panel with Lorian Hemingway, Ernest's granddaughter, who had just published her first novel, *Walking into the River.* I then accepted an invitation to be on the steering committee of the conference. The group met every month at Jake's bookstore to plan the next year's conference, to choose a major writer as Grand Master, and invite the other writers. It was through that committee that I met and got to know the Birmingham writer Fred Bonnie and became good friends with Jake Reiss.

The Alabama Library Association asked me to introduce Clifton Tolbert at their annual banquet at the Sheridan in Birmingham; his memoir, *Once Upon a Time When We Were Colored,* had been named their nonfiction book of the year. In another year I'd be standing at the same podium accepting their award for fiction book of the year for my short story collection *Somewhere in All This Green,* which Black Belt Press had brought out. The book carried a marvelous blurb on the back of the jacket from Pat Conroy.

I saw Pat again soon. His good friend Ann Rivers Siddons was the keynote writer at Southern Voices, and Pat asked if he could come back and introduce her. At a reception afterward, Pat and I were talking. "You remember that pretty blond writer you introduced me to?" he asked me. I knew he meant Sandra King Ray. At the time I introduced them, they were both going through divorces, but now both had become final. Pat had lost her contact information. I gave him her number. He said he was going to call her, and he did.

When Sandra's divorce was final, she took a job at a community college in Gadsden, north of Birmingham. Pat began driving over to see her and they'd come down to Montevallo, where we'd swim in the pool and cook seafood that Pat had brought with him from the low country. Pat is a marvelous cook; what he can do with fresh shrimp is unbelievable. We also drove over with Sandra to visit him at his house on Fripp Island, near Beaufort, South Carolina. Sandra was working on a long novel she'd begun in Montevallo called *Rise to Worlds Unknown*. I had read early drafts; it contained a married couple who were much too close to me and Loretta for my comfort. Later, when the novel would be published as *The Sunday Wife*, I was relieved to see that she had toned the characterizations down considerably; they no longer resembled us so obviously. She soon went over and moved in with Pat at his house on Fripp.

Our visits with them there are some of the high points in our lives. There were long evenings of watching Crimson Tide football or the Braves and eating raw oysters fresh from the marshes, licking the brine from the shells, talking deep into the night about writing, all of us passionate and on fire. Or driving around Beaufort with Pat pointing out places where significant things happened in his life. "That's where I made my father tell me he loved me," he would say. "That's a scene in *The Great Santini*!" I would reply. "Exactly."

I was often pleasantly exhausted by being with Pat Conroy. As reserved as I was, he was equally outgoing and talkative, spilling wit, making outrageous and iconoclastic observations, jocular, profane, and hilarious. Of a mutual friend, Pat once observed, "I never would have screwed her because I knew she'd write about how little my dick was," just as she'd done about another famous South Carolina writer.

Eighteen

My sister, Jayne, had a mastectomy. She was working at Robertson Banking Company with my old friend from the Marengo Theater, Joyce McCluskey. Pat Brasfield had remarried and had another child, a daughter. Then he and his second wife divorced. He disappeared and nobody knew where he was. Jayne married an old classmate, Mike Nettles, and they settled into the house that my father had bought for her. They were together for the rest of her life.

Meredith graduated as salutatorian of her high school class and enrolled at the University of Montevallo, which Alabama College was now called. She was on full tuition scholarship, but we insisted she not live at home. At the end of her freshman year she announced to us that she was in love and was getting married. To a boy we scarcely knew. We had raised her to be independent and think for herself, and she certainly did. She promised to work to help put herself through school, which she did. Within a year she and her husband had presented us with our first grandchild, a boy named William Jonathan Smith.

William Meredith had a stroke when he was in New York to read a commemorative poem he'd written for the centennial celebration of the Brooklyn Bridge and for several years was unable to speak or walk. Richard left a good position and went back to school to become a physician's assistant so he could care for him. He nursed William back to as good health as he would ever have again, though William walked awkwardly and spoke haltingly for the rest of his life.

In the mid-1990s, William won both the Pulitzer Prize and the National Book Award for *Effort at Speech*, his new and final book of poems. They lived in Uncasville, Connecticut. Since his days as Librarian of Congress, William had been very interested in Eastern European poetry, particularly Bulgarian. He translated a lot of Bulgarian poetry into English and guided its publication in this country. William and Richard spent a great deal of time in Bulgaria, where William was awarded the country's Vaptsarov Medal, its highest literary prize. Both of them received dual citizenship status.

One of my short stories, "The Queen of the Silver Dollar," was translated into Bulgarian and it appeared in the magazine *Orpheus*, published in Sofia and Paris. As a result, I was invited, along with Richard and William, to give a series of readings and appearances around Bulgaria. Loretta and I flew to Sofia, where we met our two friends. We checked into the Hotel Pliska for a few days before starting our tour. We began with a reading at the American Cultural Center in Sofia, then went on the road. We were provided with a large Mercedes and a driver. We attended the first graduation ceremony of American University in Blogoevgrad, where Richard had taught on a Fulbright; it was housed in an old Soviet office building from Iron Curtain days. We spoke at universities and in towns and villages all over the country, all the way up to Varna, on the Black Sea. We met poets, novelists, and visual artists and stayed at places owned by the Bulgarian Writers Union.

One of the writers we met and liked was Lada Galina, a

well-published and popular novelist, who told us on several occasions that she wanted to come to America. She did, and we welcomed her into our home, then found her a house and a job as a nanny with wealthy Birmingham doctors. Richard, William, and I all wrote letters to the state department on her behalf; she soon acquired a green card and went to work for Barnes & Noble. Lada moved to Washington, where she still resides. She has published a new novel, which she told us had characters based on me and Loretta. The book has not yet been translated into English, so we have no idea how we came across.

I was working on a new novel, this one a departure from my earlier work. It was set in Montevallo, except I called it Piper, and located it north of Birmingham rather than south. I had been reading the South American magical realists, especially Gabriel García Márquez and Mario Vargas Llosa, and the new book was written under that influence. Randall Williams had run into money problems with Black Belt. He and Wayne Greenhaw parted ways. Black Belt was foundering, and it was bought out by Al Newman, a wealthy doctor in Montgomery, who reorganized and reopened it as River City Publishers. An old friend, Ellen Sullivan, an ex-wife of Fred Bonnie's who had once published a book with Mr. Travis at Portals Press, now owned a successful new publishing house, Crane Hill Press. I would run into Ellen at literary parties around Birmingham and at the Writing Today conferences. Crane Hill had never published a novel. Ellen told me she'd like to publish one, and she wanted it to be one of mine. I showed her the new one, *A Spring of Souls*; she liked it and wanted to publish it.

I no longer worried about New York publishing houses, which I knew many people thought were the only legitimate way to publish in this country. I had long ago come to the conclusion that I would never write novels of the first rank—I was not a William Faulkner or even a Pat Conroy—and I was okay with that. It was not my gift to be a great writer or even a popular or rich one. But I could write good novels that people would consider valuable and enjoy reading. I could get the respect of my fellow writers. I had no desire for fame or big money. I came to know that the real satisfaction in writing was not getting good reviews or royalty checks (though those are nice), or even publishing, but the writing itself. If I could get to the end of the day and be gratified reading back over what I had written, could be proud of it, that was the ultimate reward. To finish a book and know that I had done it the very best I could, and it was a good book, was the important thing.

Ellen Sullivan was enthusiastic about publishing *A Spring of Souls*. She brought it out in simultaneous hardcover and trade paperback editions. She sent me to Los Angeles to Book Expo America, where I signed books for booksellers from all over the United States. I was at the same table with Eric Idle and Jamie Lee Curtis. I was the subject of a long feature in *Publisher's Daily*. Nina Costopolous, the Crane Hill publicist, set me up a daunting two-month-long book tour of the Southeast that took me to twenty-four bookstores in twenty-two cities.

As soon as I was finished with my tour, my sister, Jayne, died. She had had a recurrence of her cancer, this time in her lungs. She was only fifty-two years old. Mike Nettles was good to her and stood by her during her years of suffering. Toward the end of her life she began to drink more and more heavily. This upset her children, but I cautioned them to let her be, because she knew she was dying.

Her final days in the hospital were difficult for us. Loretta and I had promised her that we would be there for Cora, Sam, and Emily, since their father was absent, had for all practical purposes disappeared. We had taken our roles as surrogate parents very seriously. When Jayne had first been diagnosed with the terminal phase of her cancer, when it entered her lungs, we had flown out to San Diego to visit with Sam, up to Chicago to visit Emily and her husband, Cory, spent time with Cora and her husband, Allan, in Birmingham, all to assure them that they could rely on us in the future. When the end was near, everyone gathered in Demopolis. We were assured that she was not suffering, but to see her writhing on the hospital bed made that hard to believe. We were finally told that she was brain dead and there was nothing more to be done. We made the decision to let her go. When she died, I knew a large part of myself had died as well; a large chunk of our shared history was now gone, vanished into thin air. That family unit I had grown up in was now shattered, violated, and I would never be the same again.

Pat Brasfield had been out of touch with everybody for a long time. We heard rumors that he was living as a street person down on the causeway in Mobile and in Tampa, but nobody had heard directly from him in years. We were all surprised when he showed up at Jayne's funeral. He looked eighty years old, skinny and snaggle toothed, in a wrinkled Salvation Army suit. Carrying a cane. To say that his sudden appearance was awkward is an understatement. There was Mike, her widower. My mother hated Pat's guts. She felt that the way Pat had treated her daughter had put her in an early grave, and I think there is some truth to that. The difference in my feelings and my mother's was that I knew Pat couldn't help being who he was. I knew he was a kindred soul, a fellow addict. I had always known it; he was one of Captain Billy's Troopers who had lost his way and never found it. But my mother would never forgive him. Cora and Sam had both been close to him as children, and then had been betrayed by him and ignored. At the time of her mother's death, Emily hardly knew him. He was like something that had popped up out of a twisted dream.

A few weeks after the funeral, Pat called me in the middle of the night. He told me he'd gotten a letter from Jayne. The letter had been forwarded multiple times, from Tampa to Mobile to Atlanta and back again, and had only then caught up with him. He told me that Jayne forgave him for everything he'd ever done to her. He was crying. I never read the letter; I am not even sure there was ever such a thing. But it would have been like Jayne to do that, and I am comfortable in accepting that he was telling the truth. The facts, in this case, do not really matter to me. It comforts me to believe in their last connection.

Pat swore he was sober for the first time in years. He was in Huntsville, with a new job. As it happened, I was going back to Huntsville for another book signing, so I asked him to meet us at the bookstore and we'd get something to eat afterward. When he got to the bookstore, he was drunk. He had on a wrinkled white suit and a wide white panama hat, carrying his cane. He sat and insulted people waiting in line to get a book signed. He abruptly left and drove out of the parking lot in a beat-up old Volkswagen van. We would not see him again until we would visit him in prison in Virginia.

Both the hardcover and mass market paperback editions of *A Walk Through Fire* were out of print, so Crane Hill brought out a trade paperback. They also set the publication date for my new novel, *Wings of Morning*. Before the book came out, we got word that Pat had shot and killed another man in a flophouse in Richmond. He stood trial and was convicted of second-degree murder and sentenced to twenty years in a maximum-security prison in Sweetwater, Virginia, near the North Carolina state line. When I went to Raleigh-Durham to do a book signing for *Wings of Morning*, Loretta and I drove up to visit Pat while we were there. It was the last time we saw him. He seemed in robust health and was his old, witty self again, laughing and telling stories about the other prisoners. I had forgiven him.

Over the several years he was incarcerated we wrote long letters back and forth. Loretta and I sent him books. He wrote a novel, sending me sections along that I would comment on and send back. I was disappointed the book was not about prison life but a rather ordinary story of a playboy on the Gulf Coast. It was a very bad novel. Pat became ill and died in prison. Cora, Sam, and Emily scattered his ashes in Mobile Bay, off the eastern shore near Fairhope, their childhood home. He and Jayne were the first of Captain Billy's Troopers to die.

Then Winston Smith died. He had had a terrible disease, something similar to Lou Gehrig's disease, and he had been quite ill for a long time. He had resigned his position at the university and gone home to Demopolis, where he lived in his mother's house with only an old black woman to take care of him. He was a recluse; he wouldn't see many people. I once called him and told him I wanted to bring Meredith by to meet him, and he laughed and said he would scare her to death, the way he looked. He was adamant; he said he wouldn't let us in the door. Even as his illness grew worse, he still wrote me long, funny letters full of stories the old black woman had told him. The two things that always bonded us and made us friends were our mutual love of literature and our similar senses of humor. I dedicated *Wings of Morning* to his memory.

Richard received a fellowship from the Camargo Foundation in France. He and William were given an apartment on a cliff overlooking the Mediterranean in Cassis, a small village east of Marseilles, for six months. They found a tiny apartment for us and we went over to visit for several weeks. The four of us drove all over Provence, to Arles, Aix-en-Provence, and Avignon. We ate in little roadside restaurants. We cooked paella and sat on their balcony and looked out at Cassis Harbor. We visited the topless beach near their apartment, where I got my eyes filled with seemingly thousands of beautiful, bouncing French titties. Richard goaded Loretta until she, too, decided to get in the swing of things and went topless. I must say that she more than held her own.

I had begun to experience more and more pain from my arthritis. I had to stop jogging because my right knee became so painful that I could barely get out of the bed and could hardly walk on it. The doctor explained that I had no cartilage at all in my knee; it was just bone on bone. Sometimes my ankles would ache and my shoulders would grow stiff and sore. I had to occasionally use a cane. I was given anti-inflammatory medication and hydrocodone for the pain, which I knew I had to be careful with because of my addiction.

Nineteen

Against my better judgment, I agreed to write a biography, an "as told to," about a wealthy man who was married to one of my old high school friends. The couple contacted me; I resisted. They had read *Harry Reunited* and felt that it could have been about them and their friends, and they argued strongly that I was the one to write the book. They offered me an obscene amount of money to write it. I was getting on toward retirement age, I was between books, and they made the project so inviting—they would furnish me with an apartment on their estate in Mississippi, so I could do my research on his life and friends; I would have two years to complete the book, being paid in monthly installments over that period until I received the entire six-figure sum—that I agreed to do it. It was more money than I'd ever made from a book, even *A Walk Through Fire.* I think it was the first major decision I ever made in my life on the basis of money, and though I don't regret doing it, I am not proud of it.

I wound up writing a damn good book, but it is gathering dust somewhere among the papers of the man, who is now deceased, unless it has been destroyed, which is likely. I interviewed the man for countless hours, on his estate in Mississippi, at his home in Palm Beach, Florida, at his large hunting plantation in South Alabama. I interviewed his family and friends; I researched his family history—which turned out to be full of acrimony, jealousy, lawsuits, and estrangement—in newspaper morgues and at his county courthouse in Mississippi, where he was raised. He wanted his story told, "warts and all," as he put it. He had had a heart transplant; the surgeon was Dr. Mehmet Oz, at Columbia Presbyterian in Manhattan, whom I also interviewed. The man had also been intricately involved in the savings and loan scandals of some years before, though he, unlike many of his colleagues, had escaped prison.

His family—his wife and two adult children—was a total mess. I think, though they had homes all over the world (a vacation spot in Jamaica!), a private jet for jaunts to Venice, all the money anyone could ever want and then some, they were the unhappiest family I've ever known. The wife, my old high school friend, still beautiful and vibrant, had become an alcoholic (his word for her, not mine or hers), the son was obese and spent his time hunting and fishing, and the daughter, a blonde, lived a California lifestyle in Malibu. The man was dull and lifeless, with no interests other than, as he put it, "accumulating wealth." They were a living cautionary tale, a manifestation that profane and shameless "accumulation" and wanton spending did not lead to happiness. I was reminded of Dorothy Parker's acid remark: "If you want to know what God thinks of money, just look at the people he gives it to."

When I finished a draft of the book, the man was pleased. His wife was angry and felt betrayed; the adult children raged and stewed; the man's attorneys almost went postal over all he had told me about the savings and loan scandal. Everyone demanded cuts, which the man reluctantly agreed to. As per my contract, I exercised my right to withdraw my name from the project; gave him—at the request of his legal team—all my notes, drafts, tapes, and transcripts; got in my new black Miata; and went home.

I decided to retire from teaching. I had money in the bank. I had begun to experience the early onset of normal pressure hydrocephalus, though at the time I had no idea what it was. I had taught for thirty-six years, so my pension with the state retirement system would be adequate to live on. They pay teachers shit in Alabama, but we have a good retirement plan. I retired with a pension of 74 percent of my final salary. I had no qualms about leaving the university. I was burned out. At the retirement reception, everybody else's dean had prepared remarks that summarized their tenure there and at the very least tried to say something kind about them. Dean Mike Rowland had not gone to the trouble to prepare anything; he mumbled through a half-assed statement that left me seething with disappointment and anger. But Loretta and I continue to love Montevallo; we had good years there, good colleagues and friends, and many good students.

My mother was an invalid for the last five years of her life, rarely leaving the house. She began to suffer from osteoporosis and had to be hospitalized a couple of times. Finally she entered the hospital for the last time, the same hospital where my sister had died. Loretta and I went down there to be with her. Loretta would fix her hair and she would sit up in the bed in a pretty nightgown looking as attractive as she always had. She maintained her dignity to the end. When it became apparent she could never go home again, we moved her to a nursing home, which we called a convalescent home, since we wanted her to think it only temporary. We went home on Wednesday to get fresh clothes. On Friday, my birthday, the call came that she had died. She did not want to be helpless in a nursing home. I think she willed her own death.

What can a man say, what can he feel, when his mother dies? Two of the three most important women in my life were now no more. Simply gone. I had a terrifying dream that was so vivid I can recall it in every detail even today. My mother was talking to me, but she was only a head with loose skin draped around beneath her. Her body was gone. She was in front of an opening into the ground that I knew instinctively was the entrance to hell; the dirt and the withered grass around the hole were scorched and blackened. What was so astonishing to me was that the hole was *beneath the concrete front porch of the First Presbyterian Church in Demopolis*, the church where I was taught the hard, cold, and rigid tenets of Presbyterianism, where I was subjected to rituals and practices that had nothing to do with Love and Truth and everything to do with punishment and sin. My mother was not down in the hole, but I knew if I turned away for an instant, she would slide in.

The Thanksgiving after she died, we all gathered to divide my mother's nice things: her silver, china, antiques, etc. Meredith and I drove down to Demopolis. When we got there, the stuff had already been divided, and there was nothing for us. My mother had left Meredith a diamond ring because she was the only grandchild named for her. My father thought that took care of my side. I didn't want to make a scene. I called him out in the backyard. "What about me?" I asked him. He looked at me with sheer hatred. "Billy," he said, "do you want to wear your mother's clothes?" He had a demented look in his eyes, but I took it as hatred. I should have known even then that he had started his final decline, but I didn't. To me, it was just one more in a long line of injustices at his hand.

I demanded a set of my mother's china. I told my father that Loretta and I would hopefully be serving food on it for years to come, and it would mean a great deal to us if it was china that had been in our family. He made it clear that he thought I was just being greedy. He cared nothing for that kind of sentimentality and emotion. It made him angry. Meredith and I drove back to Montevallo with nothing.

Loretta and I were solidly in that season when we had to deal with aging and dying parents. Loretta's mother and father had moved to Montevallo and bought a small house. Loretta's mother developed vascular dementia. She wasted away until she died. Her father lived on for another ten years, an invalid. Loretta was the primary caregiver, and it was a very trying time for her. After my mother's death, my father declined rapidly. He wanted to stay in the house, but he was depressed. The doctor he was seeing put him on Paxil. He just sat all day, staring at the wall. Finally he decided he wanted to go out to The Willows, an assisted-living place on the Linden Highway, where some of his friends had gone. He stayed there a couple of years. I drove down to visit him often, and we gave him a ninetieth birthday party there.

Back when he had retired, when he and his partners sold the business, he had called me into the den and told me he had a lot of money, enough for the two of them to live on. He said he was dividing everything down the middle in his will: I would get one house, theirs; Jayne would get hers; and the rest of his estate would be evenly split. After my mother died, he got sick and Loretta and I went down to nurse him. He was in the hospital for several days. While there, he asked me to get his checkbook and tear out a check so he could pay the hospital. I noticed the stub of the last check written. It was to his attorney, and the memo said "New will." I knew intuitively what he had done. Jayne had, of course, died, but that wouldn't have necessitated redrawing the document. I was certain he hadn't revised his will to leave everything to me. I stewed. I confronted him. He admitted that he had had a new will drawn up. Jayne's house had been sold after she died and the money divided up between Cora, Sam, and Emily. He had sold our house, so that money was back in the estate. In the new will, he had left the estate divided equally in four parts, to Cora, Sam, Emily, and Meredith. Which effectively cut me out completely.

After I found out about the will, I was extremely angry and depressed. It was the final jab. He was not going to tell me about it, but let me find out after he died, so that he could hit me one more time from the grave. Knowing how little my father thought of me, his own son, his only heir, broke my spirit. I didn't know how I could live with it if I didn't tell him what I thought. I went down there. He yelled at me that he could leave his money to whoever he damn well pleased. I told him that yeah, I could take care of or *not* take care of whoever I damn well pleased. We had it out. He didn't seem to understand how much he was hurting me.

The next Monday he called me. He was contrite. He asked me if I could come back down there; he wanted to talk to me. I knew what he wanted. I drove down there. He said he had reconsidered and was going back to the lawyer and have the will redrawn. He spat at me, "I guess you want it all. You can have it!" No, I told him, I only want the half you originally promised. I want the price of the house off the top and the rest split evenly between me and Jayne's children. He said he would do that. He did.

We talked him into coming to Montevallo and moving into Knowlwood, a nice assisted-living facility here. He could be near his grandchildren and great-grandchildren. We could all get together in Montevallo and at my niece Cora's house on Smith Lake north of Birmingham. He seemed relatively happy and content for almost two years. After a while he developed severe dementia, and I realized he been suffering it for some time, as it increasingly grew worse. It explained some of his irrationalities.

They couldn't handle my father at Knowlwood; I was having to go over there at all hours of the night to help him search frantically for his cigarettes (he had quit smoking twenty-five years ago). I tried to move him into a nursing home, but they wouldn't take him because he was combative; he tried to hit a nurse. I didn't know what to do.

One of my old counselors, Judy Prince, who had been instrumental in getting me into rehab years before, came to the rescue. She knew someone in the geriatric psychiatric ward at UAB Hospital. She got him admitted. He no longer knew who we were. He was there three weeks before he died on Christmas Day of pneumonia. He was ninety-three years old.

A few months before he died, I was awarded the Harper Lee Award for Alabama's Most Distinguished Writer for 2007. Meredith and her husband and the kids brought my father down to Monroeville for the banquet, where I was given the award and made a speech. He looked lost, confused. On the way home he asked them, "Does that mean Billy's now chairman of the board?"

Following her retirement, Loretta began to publish more short stories. Two of them were in anthologies published by Livingston Press, a small university press at my old alma mater, now the University of West Alabama. The editor there, Joe Taylor, whom we had known along with his wife, Tricia, for years, admired Loretta's work and asked her for a collection of stories. The result was *The Ocean Was Salt*. Its publication prompted Jake Reiss to announce to the world, "Bill Cobb is now the second best writer in his household!" William Meredith was pleased that Loretta took the title of her book from the last line of his poem "The Wreck of the Thresher": "The ocean was salt before we crawled to tears."

We went to West Palm Beach to celebrate William's eighty-fifth birthday. Richard, William, and I wore our tuxedos, and Loretta dressed up and looked smashing. Three years later we would get word that William had died. I was unable to go with Loretta to New London for his funeral—I had already begun to experience more severe symptoms of NPH—but I was later feeling well enough to go to his memorial service at Connecticut College. We have continued to see Richard, both in West Palm Beach and Uncasville. He is director of the William Meredith Foundation, headquartered there.

Joe Taylor asked if Livingston Press could reissue my first two novels in trade paperback, and of course I said yes. He chose to do *The Hermit King* first, and it appeared with an introduction by Bert Hitchcock, Hargis Professor of English at Auburn University, and with five new stories that had recently been published in literary magazines. Later Livingston Press released *Coming of Age at the Y*, with a long introduction and overview of my career by Don Nobel, moderator of public television's *Bookmark* program and Professor Emeritus of English at the University of Alabama.

I continued to tend to my sobriety. Though I was not one to "systematically" do the Twelve Steps, I did see the value in some of them, especially the seventh and the twelfth steps. "Go to someone you hurt while you were drinking and apologize and ask for forgiveness." I did that with all my family and my friends. Once, when we were in Mobile, I called an old girlfriend I'd dated for a while and asked her to have lunch with me. She agreed, and at lunch I apologized for acting like such an ass at a party we both attended years ago. She did not even remember it. "Billy," she said, "you were always a perfect gentleman to me."

The twelfth step involves helping other alcoholics when they need you. I had talked numerous times to worried acquaintances. Once I was asked to go with a counselor to see one of her clients who had a problem. It was late at night, but I agreed to go and met her at a restaurant. When we got to the guy's house, the situation was volatile. He was a young man, probably around thirty. He was very drunk, had been that way for a week. His pregnant wife and little two-year-old daughter were in the living room with him. There was a loaded pistol on the coffee table. He was threatening to shoot his wife and daughter and then himself if she called anyone but the counselor. The wife and daughter were terrified. We went in. We sat down. He reached out and got the pistol, then put it back down within easy reach. The counselor and I began to talk to him, to plead with him to give us the gun and let us get him some help. I was scared shitless, but the longer and more I talked, forcefully and gently, the more relaxed I got. When I paused, the counselor took over. We sat there for more than two hours, until finally the young man broke into sobs and fell facedown on the sofa. I grabbed the pistol, and it was over. The young man agreed to go to rehab. He would go to Brookwood Lodge, in Warrior, where I had had my rehabilitation. The memories of that summer night when I had hit my rock bottom came flooding back.

Twenty

In Brookwood Hospital, that muggy night in the summer of 1984, while I still had enough alcohol coursing through me to ward off any withdrawals, an orderly wheeled me up to the top floor to a ward with a locked door and bars on the windows. I realized it was where they put the psychos, and I guessed that's where they put the rummies, too. Two hefty black nurses showed me to my room. I was relieved that they were jolly and joked with me, since I felt a little like a criminal. They helped me get undressed and told me to take a shower. I had not thought to bring anything with me, no pajamas or toothbrush. I didn't need a razor; I'd worn a full beard for years. I had no fresh clothes to put on. They gave me a toothbrush and a hospital gown.

I lay there in the dark room wide awake. I thought about Loretta and Meredith, over in Georgia, and my heart ached. I hoped that Sidney had called them. I could feel the demons creeping out of the shadows and scratching at the edges of my mind. I had never felt so lonely in my life. This must be what it feels like to die, I thought. That was something else you had to do totally alone. I thought about scenes of writhing withdrawal I'd seen in movies, *The Lost Weekend* and *The Man with the Golden Arm.* I thought about tossing in the bed burning with rheumatic fever all those years ago. For a few minutes my confused brain was convinced that I was back there again, the age Meredith was now, feeling the ragged heat smoldering all over my body, ablaze in my head.

I was trembling. Someone—a nurse, an intern, a doctor—came into the room and gave me a shot. My sleep was fitful; I lay there awake most of the night, trying to do the deep breathing exercises we'd learned in the Lamaze class before Meredith was born. Toward morning I began to dream, startling myself awake with the bizarre images that leapt forth in my mind. I don't know what I saw. I didn't see any pink elephants, and there were no spiders. Just vague forms that were people both familiar and unfamiliar. I didn't remember telling anyone about them, but once while I was in treatment, my counselor said, "Tell me about the hallucinations," and I said, "What hallucinations?" He told me that it was on my chart that I'd had hallucinations. Maybe I was talking out loud to them, and the nurses heard me.

On the one hand, that night unfolded in a haze; on the other, I remember it vividly and clearly. I had no blackout. They must have already had me on a cocktail of drugs to keep me on the edge, to prevent severe DTs and withdrawal symptoms, though I had plenty of minor ones. My entire body ached, and I bent double with the sharp pain in my abdomen, like I had swallowed a hot poker. My arms and hands trembled, but it was as though they were restrained, tied down, or I had lost all strength and the power to move them around. I felt jumpy and trembly and paralyzed at the same time. And I was covered with a cold sweat. My throat and mouth were arid and constricted, and I could smell my own unpleasant breath. Water tasted rancid and noxious. It was a long night.

The next morning a nurse brought me breakfast. Bacon and eggs. I couldn't eat. My stomach rebelled at the sight of the food. The nurse sat with me while I picked at it. The ward was very quiet. She made no reference to why I was there. I asked her how many patients were there, and she told me two. Me and an old man down the hall. "We had two more over the weekend, but they're gone on out to the lodge." I didn't ask her what the lodge was; I thought I knew. It was some kind of treatment center. And I wasn't going. I was going to get sober and go home and stop drinking. Detoxed. I had read about it.

All I did all day was lie in the bed. There was no television. I asked the nurses to bring me something to read and they said it wasn't allowed. They gave me a shot about every three hours, and I floated through the day. Later that afternoon a young doctor came in. He took my vital signs and looked in my mouth. He asked me a series of questions. Did I have blackouts? Had I ever spit up blood? Did I want to stop drinking? I answered yes to every one he asked me. He told me they wanted to send me out to Brookwood Lodge, a rehab facility out in Warrior, north of the city. They had checked my insurance and it would pay in full. It would be a minimum of thirty days. *Thirty days?!* There was no way I could do that. I had to get back to work. If I even still had a job. And I didn't want to do it. The very idea of going to one of those places filled me with revulsion. I was not one of those people. How could I have still been thinking that way? Maybe one of those apparitions that came to me in the dark night was my Uncle Russ, looking at me with swimmy eyes, his mouth twisted in a snaggled grin, murmuring, thick-tongued, "Hello, my true kinsman."

The nurses made me get up and come into a little kitchen and sit at the table to eat my supper. I had no appetite. I still felt queasy; I had thrown up the little bit of lunch I'd eaten. They were obviously giving me plenty of medication to relax me, but I was shaky. I would feel calm, sedated, then abruptly a sensation of panic would consume me. I'd feel as if I were on the verge of a seizure, as though any second my whole body would be shaking violently. But that didn't happen.

A lady came by to see me in the evening. Her name was Marion

Cranford, and she was a counselor with Brookwood Lodge. She was about fifty, a no-nonsense woman who got right to the point. If I valued my life, I would go into rehab, she told me. If I didn't, I was going to die. Drinking the way I'd been doing was slow suicide. She told me to think about it overnight and tell her in the morning. They could arrange for me to be taken right out there. I told her if I decided to go, I'd need to go home to get clothes and toilet articles. She laughed. "No," she said, "trust me, you don't want to go back home." She said that would be taken care of. I told her I wanted to call my wife. "No phone calls," she said. "You'd think I was in the goddam jail," I said. She laughed again. "You checked yourself in," she said.

I didn't sleep very much at all that night. I just lay there in that still, empty quiet, desperately willing the time to pass. I could have set my watch by the injections. They came with regularity all night long. By morning I had made up my mind. I would surrender. I would give myself over to whatever lay ahead and simply trust. Looking back now, I see that single, simple choice as the most important of my life. I think what I knew then—as Marion said—was that I would die soon. Or I would recover. I would let them take me and do whatever they were going to do, without resisting. It sounds simple now, but it was the most difficult thing I'd ever done. I think with that willingness to surrender I was taking the first tiny step in making myself over, in controlling my disease. It was like closing my eyes and jumping off the high dive when I was a child, confident the water would cushion me. But this time I didn't quite know what was down there. And I was scared. I hadn't ever minded being alone; now I was *truly* alone, among sober strangers who seemed to be existing on a slightly different plain from mine, moving at an almost imperceptibly altered pace.

It was late in the morning when they came to get me in my room. One of the nurses had a fresh pair of khakis and one of my shirts, socks, fresh underwear. It hardly registered on me that they were *my* clothes. My body was not mine; I was dressing someone else. My movements were slow and deliberate, as if I were under water. When they escorted me out the door with the bars on the window, into the hallway, there stood Loretta and Meredith. They had both been crying, but they had stoic, forced-cheerful expressions on their faces. They were being strong for me. It melted my heart. There was a young man standing behind them; I was confused, disoriented. I didn't know who he was. I thought he was with them. I thought that in the little time I'd been away, the world as I'd known it had changed in disparate ways and I was on the outside looking in. I wanted to die, or at least to flee. Then the young man stepped forward and picked up my suitcase, and I realized he was my escort to wherever I was going.

I hugged them both. They clung to me for a long time. Then we straightened up. I was crying; I didn't want to leave them. But I was ready to be led. The young man carried my suitcase—which Loretta had packed for me—down the hall. I looked back and Loretta and Meredith were watching me, standing in front of the door with the bars on the window. I waved and they waved back. I felt as though I were disappearing, fading away from the earth as I knew it.

The young man's name was Tommy. He drove me out the interstate, chattering. He told me he had been a patient at Brookwood Lodge and now worked there. He thought I was doing the right thing. I would never regret it. I didn't believe him. I thought about yanking the door handle, jumping out of the car. My breathing was shallow. The greenery beside the highway seemed oddly askew, the color not quite right, as though the leaves were covered with a thin layer of fine dust. It was like my world had gone out of focus. Nothing would ever be quite right again. We left the interstate for a two-lane road, then turned off down a narrow drive through thick woods. Rounding a curve, I saw my new home for the next thirty days, sitting in a clearing. It might as well have been in the north woods of the Yukon.

In a kind of walking coma, I got out of the car and was led into the building. I was checked into the detox unit, a medical clinic located at one end of a long administration building. At the other end was the lobby and public entrance, and in between were meeting rooms, offices, and the cafeteria. I was in a double room, but there was nobody in there with me. I was examined, blood taken. I was given pills in a little wax paper cup. I wandered out into the common room, with sofas, a television set. There was a woman sitting there, about my age, in a bathrobe and slippers. "Hi," she said, "I'm Jackie." "Bill," I said. I sat down. "Mind if I watch TV?" I asked. She laughed. "Shit," she said, "no TV. The fucking thing's a VCR." There was a stack of videotapes of movies. She saw me looking at them. "You've seen 'em all," she said, "but you can watch one if you want to." I didn't want to. I just sat there fidgeting.

She had a nice smile, but a sad one. She, too, looked like she'd been crying. She was just sitting in silence, staring at the wall. I looked around. There was no reading matter. A nurse brought my lunch in from the cafeteria on a tray. A cheeseburger with fries. I ate about half of it. It was not bad, the best food I'd had in a while. Nurses in white uniforms came and went, paying no attention to me and Jackie. After what seemed like a long time, I asked her, "What do we do?" She looked angry. "What do you mean, what do we fucking do?" she said bitterly.

I didn't say anything more. The afternoon passed in a stultifying boredom. I could not believe I was actually there. Later, a man a little younger than me came in. He was tall, with straight blond hair and little clear rim glasses. He, too, wore a bathrobe and slippers. I could see pajama legs sticking out of the bottom. He told me his name was Don. He was much more talkative than Jackie. He told us that he was going up to a cottage tomorrow. He seemed genuinely happy about it. I asked and was told that the patients lived in group cottages, three for men, three for women. There were about twenty in each one. Don said that he was a dentist. Jackie said she was a travel agent. I was relieved they weren't bums.

The next day, Sunday, was visiting day. Out the window of the common room I could see people all over the lawn. We could not go out there. (I wouldn't have.) Don, Jackie, and I watched *Shane.* I watched the people on the grass—couples, groups of three or four—trying to figure out which ones were the patients. One of the nurses left the outside door to the lawn open when she went out. I saw someone familiar out there, a muscular young man. He was looking at me. He had been my student, and I'd known him outside class. I knew him pretty well. His name was George. He had graduated six or seven years ago. I thought he was an English major and I was astonished that he was working there. He barreled right in the door. "Mr. Cobb!" he said, a big grin on his face. "What are you doing here?" I asked. "What the fuck you think I'm doing here?" he said, smiling broadly. He was glad to see me. He rolled on the balls of his feet. His shoulders and upper arms were thick, as if he were a weight lifter. I was confused, stunned to see someone I knew, someone who could see me in the detox unit and know the truth. I was embarrassed. If he didn't work here, he must be visiting somebody. Who? My mind raced.

"I'm in for six weeks minimum," he said. "Cocaine." He laughed. He glanced out the door. "Listen, I gotta run. I'll see you round, okay? Maybe we'll be in the same cottage." He disappeared back outside. I was reeling. My expectations had been fractured. I didn't know what to expect next. We sat idly in the commons room, surrounded by the rubbing alcohol smell from the nurses' station and the faint scents of cooking from the cafeteria. I could hear the people's voices, the laughter. The scene was not somber, but happy, upbeat. Like a dinner on the ground or a lawn party. I felt isolated from it; my ravaged, damaged brain was making me believe I was locked up. My hands were shaking so badly I had trouble lighting my pipe. I bummed a cigarette from Jackie. She was puffing away like a madwoman. Then it was late afternoon and the people were all gone and we were once again immersed in silence. We just sat there like zombies. "They don't tell you anything," Jackie said bitterly. "It must be part of the goddam treatment."

The next morning I was given a thorough physical examination. Later that afternoon I was visited by a serious young man with black hair and rimless glasses. He was Ken Lyles. He told me he'd be my counselor during my treatment. I was to be sent up to a cottage the next day. I would have an interview with Dr. Jack White, the medical director of Brookwood Lodge, before I moved in. I was feeling much better, but my nerves were still raw. In spite of all the tranquilizers they were giving me, I was still suffering from anxiety. That night I couldn't sleep. I was overwrought about living for a month with men I didn't know, some of whom, I learned after talking with George, were in the Lodge for addictions other than alcohol.

About midnight someone threw on the bright lights of my room. Another man was brought in and put in the other bed. He was a little older than me, balding, potbellied. He was dragged stumbling into the room, passed out on his feet, by three of his friends, followed by an orderly and a nurse. I heard one of the men tell the nurse that the man had drunk a quart of Early Times Bourbon on the drive from Montgomery. That's the only way they would have ever gotten him there, he said. They left him sprawled on the bed, a sheet over him, and retreated, shutting off the light. They didn't seem to have even noticed that I was there. The man began to snore, to breathe heavily and snort, to mumble and groan. He continued that all night, and I didn't sleep at all.

Dr. Jack White was a thin, wiry man in his late fifties or early sixties. He sat behind his desk, peering at me through his glasses. He gave me a stack of books (one was the Big Book, the AA Bible) and told me that if I completed the program, there was an 80 percent chance I'd recover. He said I would have to work hard and apply myself diligently while I was there, in the classes and counseling sessions, and after leaving I would have to go to a Continuing Care program at Brookwood Hospital for two years. I would also, with the help of my counselor, commit myself to a plan of regular attendance at AA meetings for at least two years. I would stay sober without a relapse. That was the program: all of it. For people who could do that, he said, they would, at the end of the two years, have that 80 percent chance.

It was quite a task, and I couldn't imagine myself finishing it. Dr. White said I would have to own the reality that I had a serious, chronic disease. It was not enough to simply put the stopper in the bottle. For the greatest majority of alcoholics, merely stopping drinking was only the first step. He told me that if you sobered up a horse thief, all you had was a sober horse thief. I didn't know what he meant. My mind was foggy from lack of sleep. He briefly outlined the treatment: There would be group therapy and individual therapy; there would be lectures, films, videos; I would be required to keep a daily diary, logging my activities. Finally, I needed to know that in cases where the patient quit and left before the end of treatment, there was a strong chance that the insurance company would not pay. And the cost was substantial.

The cottages were two-story modern buildings with wings of bedrooms built around a large, high-ceilinged central common area with a kitchen. They were nicely appointed, with comfortable furniture scattered around. There were two men in each room. My first roommate was an older man from Sand Mountain, up in the northern part of the state, named Clyde. He was as country as they came; he even wore overalls. He snored so loud that I had to go out and sleep on one of the sofas; I slept fitfully on the sofa, worried that I was breaking some rule, some protocol that I didn't know about. I lay awake for long stretches, so raw and irrational I imagined that addled, drug-ravaged street people might attack me any minute. I didn't know what was in store for me in this strange place or who was in the cottage, other than Clyde; I was all alone in the dark, and my imagination ran wild. I was terrified of every shadow. My pulse was pounding; my blood pressure must have been sky high. I was paralyzed from lack of sleep. My hands were shaking. I had given up all control, and what I wanted more than anything was a drink. That was the only thing that could calm me. I would never have another drink! What if I never got another night's sleep? The morning light began to seep in around me. I tiptoed back to my room. Clyde still lay there, mouth wide open, still snoring. I stood there for a long time, looking at him. He had lost most of his teeth. His face was red; his thin green-tinted hair looked painted on his pinkish scalp. What was *I* doing here? I was a writer, a professor of English, a husband and a father, an educated, sophisticated man, and here I was, in a drunk tank with people such as him? I was a good person, but I was a fucking drunk! In the cool, early morning stillness I wanted to break down and cry. I could feel it welling up in me, stinging the backs of my eyes.

My friend and former student George was in my cottage. He greeted me and walked with me to the cafeteria for breakfast. I was beginning to get my appetite back; I had always been especially fond of breakfast and this one was good. Scrambled eggs, grits, crisp bacon, sausage, hot fluffy biscuits, and fruit. Gallons of coffee, all decaf, George informed me. We were allowed no caffeine at all. The men ate on one side of the cafeteria, the women on the other. I saw Jackie over there; she still had on her bathrobe.

Don was also one of my cottage mates. The rest were a varied bunch. A large number of them were like Clyde, from so far back in the sticks they could barely speak English. Some were sullen and unfriendly; others were jovial and came on too strong to me. I was uptight, unsure of myself. Self-conscious. There were young men: Ralph, a used car salesman; Wayne, an insurance salesman. And boys, some of them right off the streets, acting as though they were still hopped up on crack. They were raucous and loud. There was a lot of horseplay and kidding around. These were men I never would have chosen to be around. They were men I had little in common with, except for one thing. We were all addicts. Addiction was our lowest common denominator and it had brought us all together, like it or not.

The group was constantly changing as men rotated in and out, some completing their rehab, others walking out in the middle.

During my thirty-three-day stay, the core group was substantially the same, with Don and George, who was now an attorney, and after a couple of days Foy, the man who had been brought into my room in detox. He was an amiable, intelligent man who was a state senator, probably one of the last liberal Democrats to serve in the Alabama legislature. The four of us became close friends. Some of the younger guys started calling me "Professor," Don "Doc," and Foy "Senator." Ken demanded that they quit. "He's Bill," he said, pointing to me and then Don and then Foy. "And he's Don. He's Foy. No titles here! We're all the same."

Our days fell into a routine. In the mornings we had group therapy with Ken Lyles in one of the "recovery rooms" that opened off the commons. In the afternoons we had our private sessions, when we had to go over our diaries with Ken. He was a good counselor; he got me to begin to talk about my feelings, to force me to open up to myself. He made us be brutally honest to the other men in the group sessions, to call anybody who tried to bullshit, which got extremely agitated at times, resulting in fights that Ken had to break up. There was a lot of anger. And I cried in front of other men for the first time in my life. I was not the only one to do it. But there was also delirious laughter; one day we each had to talk about the people we had hurt, and Clyde, my roommate, when it was his time to speak, said, "Well, I fucked my wife in the ass one time." The room exploded with cackles and catcalls. On another occasion Ken was talking about our libidos. "Is that your dick?" Ralph asked. He was close.

Clyde went home and Ken put Don and me in a room together. Don didn't snore, so my sleeping improved. I was eating well and beginning to feel more rested. And as the alcohol continued to seep from my system, I felt stronger physically. We had to exercise every day. We had classes that showed us, through videos and charts, what alcohol had done to our brains. We learned we had brain damage that would never go away. We watched movies like *The Days of Wine and Roses* and *A Sensitive, Passionate Man*. Without telling us, they constantly changed the mealtimes and the time we had to line up for medications. They were forcing us to confront frustrating things we couldn't control.

We were free in the evenings to sit around in the commons and smoke, drink decaf coffee, and talk. There was a television set, but like the set in the detox clinic, it was not hooked up to receive programs. We could not watch television, listen to the radio, or read newspapers. We got to watch one movie a week in the cottage, and there was much arguing and fussing over choosing one from the list of old pictures that were available. Many of them the same ones I had seen in detox. A favorite was *Poltergeist*. We watched it twice. We could have microwave popcorn on that occasion. On Saturday nights we were allowed our one phone call of the week, not to exceed ten minutes.

You weren't allowed to have visitors until you'd been there for at least ten days. Loretta and Meredith came the second Sunday I was in the cottage. We sat in the cafeteria and Meredith drank Hi-C. We walked around the grounds. I introduced them to my new friends. Meredith brought me a Trivial Pursuit game and Loretta brought me my chess set. They had to turn them in at the office to be inspected before they were delivered to me in the cottage. All gifts and packages had to go through that process. Ken told me that people were always trying to smuggle in a bottle. You could not have mouthwash, shaving lotion, even alcohol-based roll-on deodorants. No books or magazines. If we wanted to read, we had to read the Big Book or one of the texts on addiction and recovery. You could write and receive letters; I wrote long ones, to Norman and Sid, to Jayne, to Loretta, to Meredith, to my folks. I spent so much time writing letters that one day Ken came and peered over my shoulder. "You're not writing fiction, are you?" he asked. He didn't want me even *thinking* about writing fiction.

The next Sunday my folks and Jayne drove up from Demopolis. Loretta and Meredith didn't come. You could have a maximum of three visitors at one time, and all visitors had to be put on a list and cleared ahead of time. They were very strict. My mother and father told me they were proud of me for what I was doing. My sister and I went for a walk together. She and Pat had divorced and she had moved back to Demopolis with the three children. She cried and told me that she had had Pat put in jail for nonpayment of his child support. I kept thinking, here I was in the drunk tank and Jayne's husband was in jail. What did our parents do to deserve two such sterling offspring? *Plenty*, I was realizing more and more. We were a family, and we talked a lot at the Lodge about the "family mobile," about how the action of one piece affects the rest of the structure. Alcoholism is a family disease. Dr. White, in one of his lectures, had told us that our "enablers," our "significant others," were just as sick as we were.

The last week was "family week," and our "significant others" were urged to come and stay on campus the entire time. There were special facilities for them. We did not stay together, and though they ate in the cafeteria, they were at different tables. We saw them only in group therapy sessions every day. George's father came. Jackie had her father, too. Don's knockout girlfriend, Sherry, who had written him graphic, pornographic love letters, which he had read aloud in the commons, was in attendance for him. Foy and I had our wives. Loretta looked terrific. She had a new kinky perm. She had never been prettier. I was overjoyed to see her, but bothered by her standoffishness.

We had been warned that the reentry would be difficult and painful, but I was not prepared for Family Week. We sat around in a circle in folding chairs. I had not expected such anger. The significant others were prepared to tell us what shits we'd been, and with Ken's encouragement, they did. Then it was our turn. I told Loretta that she'd been my enabler, that we were in it together, that she was a "co-alcoholic," and she was furious. She cried and called me an "asshole." Everybody all took turns cataloging and listing all the crappy things we'd done to each other, all the lies, all the cheating. To this day I don't know how Ken Lyles kept us from killing each other. We got it all out on the table. Day after day. Toward the end of the week we began to comfort one another, reaching out to other people, to each other.

A remarkable thing was happening. There was a profound connection in that room. In contrast to that pale and insubstantial "brotherhood" espoused by those frat men back during my college years, this was real human bonding, something that those people probably would never experience unless they, too, had had the shit kicked out of them and were forced to stand emotionally raw before the world. This bunch of strangers who five weeks before had not even known each other were all naked, stripped down to the bone, our souls bared. All pretense was gone. There were no disguises, no masks. There was nothing left to hide. And we were all better people for it. We were grateful that we'd been privileged to experience it.

I found the kind of love there in that group that I think Christ was talking about in the Gospels; that recovery room was what the Presbyterian Church *should* have been for me when I was a boy, all those years ago. This seemed to me what religion, what Christianity, should be about. We had walked through the valley together, we had experienced Good Friday together, and we were coming out into a new Easter. We were the ones being "born again," and to hell with all those pious Christians who would look down their noses at this bunch of addicts and drunks and their neurotic enablers. I understood, for the first time in my life, what "Love thy neighbor as thyself" really meant. These were no longer just words to me.

When Loretta drove me through that gate out of the Brookwood Lodge compound, I was as terrified and frightened as I'd ever been in my life. Now it was just me on the tightrope, without the comfortable net of the Lodge, and I would succeed or fail on my own. I knew I had the support of Loretta and the rest of my family, and of my friends and colleagues, but I couldn't do it for them. I knew if I had it in my mind that I was recovering for anybody else,

I would grow to resent them. I had been warned to change my playmates and playgrounds. I knew I didn't want to stop socializing with my friends, and I didn't know how I'd deal with that. I dreaded the first time someone offered me a drink. I had told Ken that Loretta liked to drink and I didn't think my allergy to alcohol should interfere with her pleasure. I wanted her to keep liquor in the house and offer drinks to our friends. Ken told me that was a recipe for disaster. Some members of AA went to a meeting every day, sometimes two. I told Ken I wasn't going to do that. We compromised: I signed a pledge for three meetings a week. I already knew how difficult that would be for me, as we'd had AA meetings in the lodge. I found them tedious in the extreme.

I was trying to buy into "one day at a time." I did not—*should* not—have to think about not having a drink for the rest of my life, a daunting, depressing prospect; I could wake up every morning and tell myself that I was not going to drink *that day*. One day was not as overwhelming as a lifetime. Surely I could make it through one day. And if I made it through that one, then I could start over on the next one. I was determined to give it a try. Those single days eventually became thirty years.

I knew that I was burying an old life, that in a very real sense a part of me had died, and I would go through all the stages of grief. I wondered if I would ever be able to write fiction again, if my creativity and imagination would be so muffled by sobriety that I would be hopelessly blocked. It was almost like learning to walk again, and I was not at all confident that I could do it.

Twenty-one

But I could. And I did. Since that summer I have written some very good books and plays and short stories—as well as the occasional essay. I have gotten good reviews and received some accolades, like the Harper Lee Award. The single most significant thing I've learned about myself over the years is that I would write fiction whether anybody was ever going to read it or not. Of course, I still wish for my writing to have a larger audience, but that is not the important thing. The writing itself is the important thing, and I am dependent on no one but myself for that gratification. It's nice if somebody reads it and likes it, but it's not necessary. Because I've already gotten the ultimate pleasure from it by completing it, and everything else is just gilding. Sure, as a writer you want to be rewarded. You want recognition and respect. But fundamentally what you need is to be honest and true.

In 2005, five years after my retirement from teaching, I began work on a new novel, *The Last Queen of the Gypsies*. It was a difficult novel to write, with two main characters—two protagonists—who don't see each other until the very end. The time sequences of the chapters, switching back and forth from one main character to the other, were giving me trouble. When I'd get blocked, I'd work on researching and drafting a historical novel about the Creek Indian War. Both books seemed to be giving me more of a challenge than anything I'd ever written. It was difficult to pull them out of my mind. Perhaps, I thought, I was just getting old. There were days when I couldn't seem to focus very well, and my progress became slower and slower. Then I began to experience falls; I would lose my balance and the next thing I knew I'd be on the floor or on the ground. I fell in the living room and broke a lamp that had belonged to my mother. The stairs in the house became treacherous for me to maneuver.

The worst thing was my brain. My thought processes seemed to flutter and fragment. There would be a day in the week when even the simplest things, like turning on the television, did not make any sense to me. I would forget how to do it. And words would not come to me, ordinary, everyday things, names, just whatever came next. My thinking became as halting as William's speech. The doctors I was seeing did not know what was going on with me. My primary care physician incompetently told me I "was just getting old." But by this time I knew it was something more.

One summer day when I was working on the pool, emptying the skimmer, I tried to rise from a squatting position and lost my balance and fell on the pool deck, causing some pretty terrible skin burns from the concrete. It registered with me then that I had been unable to regain my balance as I tried to stand, but I passed it off as my shifting center of gravity as I gained more and more weight.

One day later in the summer I was home alone, doing the laundry. Loretta had gone into Birmingham to take our granddaughter Sara Beth shopping. We loved our old house, a rambling, drafty barn with decks on the back overlooking the pool and the woods, but it was on two levels, the first floor or the basement level and then the living quarters upstairs. The washer and dryer were downstairs, as was my study or office, a cluttered, book-lined enclave where I had composed countless short stories and most of my novels up to then. I was on my way up the basement stairs with two batches of hangers of fresh laundry, one in each hand, and almost to the top when I suddenly fell backward and slid down the carpeted stairs and banged the back of my head on the concrete block wall. I was contorted, wedged in at the bottom of the staircase, covered in clean shirts. For a few minutes I couldn't move; I was disoriented but quickly realized I was not badly hurt.

After working my way out and carefully getting myself and the clothes up to the second floor, I was able to think about what had just happened to me. It was as though the next step of the stairs had been jerked away from me and my foot had gone into air, propelling me backward. When Loretta and Sara Beth got home, they changed into their bathing suits downstairs and went out to the pool; I was upstairs watching a Braves game. Eventually Sara Beth came in to get something cold to drink. From the refrigerator across the room she said, "Papa! What happened to your head?!" I reached up and touched the place where I'd crashed into the wall, and my fingers came back bloody. "I fell down the stairs," I said. I was hoping nobody would notice, would leave me in peace, since I knew I wasn't badly hurt.

Of course, Loretta would have nothing but a trip to the emergency room, in spite of my protests. I had all the tests, CT scan, EKG, everything the doctors could think of, and they could find nothing. No concussion, nothing. They sent me home.

I had been seeing an orthopedist for years for a steadily worsening arthritis condition that affected my legs, feet, and lower back. I had had several epidural pain blocks already, and I went back to him, suspecting that the condition of my back had somehow caused me to lose my balance. He told me I had no strength in my left leg and ordered another steroid shot. I had intermittent back pain for the next few months, nothing I couldn't live with, but I was troubled by a persistent lack of balance. It wasn't dizziness. I never felt faint or confused. I staggered a few times and began to use a cane when I went out. One day I was working in my studio and went out to get the mail. On the way back I came through the back gate. Before I got to the door, I fell on the sidewalk. I was on my side and back, jammed against the house. I tried to roll over, but I couldn't. It was as though I had no control over my body. It was both humiliating and terrifying. After trying several ways to get me up, Loretta had to call Lee Wallace, our next-door neighbor of many years, to come over and help her.

My primary care physician, Jonathan Merkle, was still baffled and told me that my balance problem was probably something I'd just have to live with for the rest of my life; he made no recommendation that I see any kind of specialist other than the orthopedist I was already seeing. I used my cane all the time then. One day, coming back from a trip to Connecticut for our dear friend William Meredith's memorial service and a visit with Richard Harteis, Loretta and I ran into Dr. Charles Clark in the Atlanta Airport. Dr. Clark is a neurosurgeon who had operated on Loretta's neck some years previously, and we were pleased with the result. We struck up a conversation and he asked about my cane. When I told him my story, he said that I should come see him, that my problem was very likely not orthopedic but neurological.

So I began to see him. He sent me over to a neurologist, who tested me for Parkinson's disease. My MRI showed arthritis in my lower back pinching nerves in my hips. My CT scan showed something in my brain that looked like a shadow, or a smear on the film. Dr. Clark determined that I had a cyst-like formation in my brain, suggested we watch it for six months and then a year and see if it grew, and ordered yet another epidural pain block. He was comfortable that it was not more critical than that, though during the period I was seeing him, he decided that I had a benign tumor, not a cyst, which didn't make a hell of a lot of difference to me except that I didn't like the word *tumor*.

I was getting no treatment other than for the pain in my back, so I didn't, of course, get better. In fact, I got progressively worse. My cognitive abilities began to deteriorate. I was forgetful. I would drive downtown and then forget why I went. And I began to develop incontinence, which eventually got so bad that I quit going to my grandson Jonathan's baseball games because I couldn't make it to the bathroom and would embarrass everybody by pissing all over myself. The same for football games.

I could no longer handle the stairs in our house, so we determined that we'd have to move and find a place all on one level. It almost killed us both. We'd been in the house over forty years. It was our first and only house, the one Meredith, our daughter, grew up in. When we found it, years earlier, it was on a dirt road outside Montevallo with just a few houses around it. It was for sale at $21,900, a daunting sum for us then, and it was an unusual house, which greatly appealed to us. Half the house was one big room with a cathedral ceiling that contained the kitchen, the dining area, and the living area. There was a huge deck that ran the length of the house in the back, with two sets of sliding glass doors opening into both the living area and the master bedroom at the rear. On the front side, two other bedrooms with a bath between. Nothing behind the house but woods. We had improved it over the years, made it truly our home, and put in a pool when Meredith was a teenager. And suddenly we had to move.

I was depressed. I had been working on the two novels off and on for several years, not making much progress with either. I completed a draft of *The Last Queen of the Gypsies*, but I just couldn't get it right, and the state of my health was preventing me from finishing it. I had also written an early draft of the historical novel of the Creek Indian War, *The Vineyards of Eden*, but I didn't have the energy nor the clearheadedness to finish either one of them.

My speech was erratic; sometimes I would stumble over words, searching for the right ones. On some days my dementia made my mind seem strangely hollow, as though my brain were full of nothing but fog. It was terrifying, because I knew it would only get worse. I began seeing Dr. Cleve Kinney, a geriatric psychiatrist at UAB; he tested me, one of those tests with a series of questions, then little brightly colored plastic pieces to fit together to match an illustration. I could do very little of it. But I only had "mild dementia." He assured me that I didn't have Alzheimer's, but I might well develop it over time. I had to struggle to beat back the old depression that has haunted me all my life.

We were getting ready for a trip to Louisiana for a Crawfish Festival with friends. During the night I heard a loud thump, went up front and looked around, turned on the lights, and looked around outside. Nothing. The next morning I discovered that the ceiling had fallen in the downstairs bathroom and water was dripping all over the carpet. The repairman got the water shut off and inspected everything; he determined that the dishwater upstairs, almost directly over the bathroom, had been sloppily installed so that water was leaking from the connections and probably had been since the dishwater was installed the previous November. It was then April. He showed me how the floor in the kitchen area was buckling under the hardwood. Part of the floor would have to be replaced. He agreed to the repairs and said he'd give me an estimate when we got back from Louisiana.

The festival was near Lafayette. We visited with our good friends Clai Rice and his wife, Lydia, who had lived in Montevallo. Clai for several years was the linguist in the English Department. We listened to the music at the festival, ate Cajun food. Loretta and Clai took a dance lesson, and Lydia and I watched from the sidelines. Lydia had finished her PhD and was teaching in the women's studies program at Louisiana, Lafayette. We were planning my trip to Lafayette the following fall, which I had agreed to a year previously. I was to be the keynote speaker for the town's "Big Read Program," in which everybody was reading *To Kill a Mockingbird*. I was to talk about Harper Lee, talk about my own treatment of racial issues in Alabama in *A Walk Through Fire*, and give a reading and meet with classes at the University of Louisiana at Lafayette. We told them about the dementia, and they said, "Come on, we'll handle it together."

After the festival, we went on to New Orleans with friends. Over my strenuous objections, we walked from the Acme Oyster House all the way to Preservation Hall, a good six long blocks. It was packed, nowhere to sit. It was almost closing time, so we listened to the music for a while, then started back to the hotel. My back had gotten quite stiff in the crowd, and when we got back outside, I couldn't walk. My legs just folded under me. With my friend Bobby Hughes on one side and Loretta on the other, and the others following noisily behind, we hobbled back to the hotel. Why we didn't have sense enough to get a taxi, I don't know. Loretta went directly to a bellman and ordered a wheelchair. The people on the street probably thought I was drunk, but I was the only completely sober one in the bunch. I spent most of the next day in our room.

When we got home, it was time to deal with the state of the house. We were determined to move to a new place and do it quickly. I had to pull myself up when I mounted the stairs, and going down was treacherous. We had to sell our house quickly, but before we could move on, we had to get it in shape, so the men started in on the repairs. It was chaotic. Loretta gave me the task of arranging and packing our books. I could not do it. I would sit staring at a book for the longest time, unable to determine whether it should be packed or disposed of.

In the meantime, we were frantically looking at houses. Our longtime friend Janice Seaman, a realtor, found us one with everything on one floor that we liked, that was in the same neighborhood as Meredith and our two grandchildren. We made our decision in one afternoon and signed the papers nine days later. I was in such sad shape that I could not help much with the moving.

I solved one problem by calling the archivist at the library at Auburn University, where my papers and manuscripts reside in the Alabama Writers Collection. He came and took a van load of material back to Auburn, thus clearing out my studio. We solved another by giving our collection of autographed books to the Carmichael Library at Montevallo. It included several hundred volumes, many by well-known writers; eventually, they put them into the William and Loretta Cobb Collection, housed in handsome glass-front bookcases given by the alumni association, where they will stay forever, or until a new librarian comes in one day and, not knowing who the hell William and Loretta Cobb were, throws them all out.

It was our first newly built house, our first neighborhood with covenants, which I did not take to. Meredith begged me to just get a mailbox like everybody else, to those exact specifications, and not make an ass of myself by resisting. She pointed out that we no longer lived in our big old house in the woods where nobody gave a flying shit whether we kept up the yard or not. My rebellious spirit was subdued, by the balance issues, by my dementia, and by my tendency to piss myself like a six-month-old. I quietly acquiesced and became a suburbanite. Without books or music. A new, never-before-lived-in brick house with walk-in closets and stink fans in the bathrooms. For the first few months I felt like I was living in a fucking hotel.

Janice sold our house almost immediately, to a young couple who obviously saw the same charm in the place that we had. The house was paid for, so the money was all profit and gave us a bit of liquidity, which helped us to buy the new one. But I was still very depressed. I know now that I've been depressed—clinically depressed—most of my adult life, from my adolescent teen years through my years of active alcoholism, even throughout my long sobriety.

During that moving summer of 2009, our lives looked pretty bleak. My cognitive powers were deteriorating. I had to wear Depends if we went out. I fell several times and could not get up: once when I had foolishly gone out to get the mail without my cell phone and lay on the driveway in the blazing sun for a quarter of an hour before Loretta, who was dressing in the back of the house, missed me and looked out and came flying out to rescue me, and once in the kitchen, on the tile floor. Both times we had to call Meredith to come and help me get up. Loretta couldn't lift me by herself, but Meredith, in spite of her being only 5-feet-1-inch tall and 105 pounds—she works out, runs, does yoga—could get me up by kneeling down, putting our backs together, slowly standing up using each other for leverage. At least the floor was much cooler than the concrete driveway in the sunshine.

I went up to St. Vincent's Hospital in Birmingham for physical therapy. I went twice a week, and they put me in a pool and directed me through exercises. I had a home health care nurse who came to the house and helped me stretch and exercise. Nothing seemed to do any good.

All of this was shattering any self-confidence I had left. I couldn't write, I couldn't fish, I was no fun to go anywhere with. I felt I couldn't do much of anything anymore. Loretta and I knew that this probably meant the end of our traveling together, since a transatlantic flight would be very difficult for me, and this in itself was disheartening. I was getting used to the house; thank goodness Jonathan could mow the small patch of grass that was our lawn now. In the old house I was accustomed to something going wrong every other day, plumbing or electrical, the pool, the roof, but the new house seemed to have no flaws at all, and that was good. But this house had not an ounce of the character of our old house. The old barn was comfortable and right, in spite of its drafts, its eccentricities, its sticky doors, and ancient bathrooms with fixtures from the early sixties. It was a good house. This is a house I could never love. If you can really love a house. And I know you can, because I loved our old one. Deeply.

When September came, we began to turn our attention to our trip back to Louisiana. I had been committed to the gig for a year, and I knew they were counting on me. And they were paying me a very nice honorarium. And I did want to see Lydia and Clai again. Just being around them made me feel better.

I was doubtful about going. Sometimes I could barely stand up, and I was afraid of humiliating myself in front of people, especially Lydia and Clai. But I thought my mind, if not my body, was up to it. I insisted on starting out driving. We made it as far as Meridian, Mississippi, before I had trouble. We had stopped for lunch at a Red Lobster, a place familiar to me from when I lived briefly in Meridian for that writing project about the rich folks that I undertook around the turn of the millennium. I had a rather messy and embarrassing episode in the men's room, which dampened our enthusiasm for the trip. So Loretta drove the rest of the way—in my old Mercedes—without further incident. We met Clai and Lydia and they took us to our hotel, where we checked in and got settled.

The "Lafayette Big Read" celebration was set up to last a week. My first duty was a panel, with several local people and Mary Ann Wilson, the chairperson of Women's Studies at the university, a classmate of Loretta's and one of my former students, a brilliant woman who had the good sense to hire Lydia.

The panel was held in one of the public libraries in Lafayette, a lovely small city in Acadia, or Cajun Country, near Baton Rouge, and was well attended. It came off without a hitch. I learned one thing: Mary Ann told us all that when Lippincott had first published Harper Lee's novel, they had marketed it as a young adult title. I didn't know that, or I had forgotten it, but it explained a lot to me. Frankly, I don't think too much of the novel, and even less of its author. I always felt that she was snobbish to other Alabama writers, unwilling to meet people who admired her and idolized her, unwilling to lend her personal inspiration to aspiring students of the craft or even to speak or autograph books. (Her recent legal suit against the little courthouse museum in Monroeville for "infringing" on her copyright, after the town has supported her to the point of deification, only strengthens my opinion.)

After the panel, we went with Clai and Lydia, Mary Ann, and

some of their colleagues and friends to eat Cajun food and listen to Cajun music, as we did every night thereafter, always having an early bedtime for my benefit. I felt good. People were saying nice things about my work, and just being around Lydia and Clai really pepped me up and filled me with energy.

The next morning I went down to breakfast before Loretta was ready. While I was standing in the buffet line, I suddenly became disoriented and began to list to the side. I was not dizzy or light-headed. I just felt that I was falling over and there was nothing I could do to stop it. I didn't think I would pass out and there was no pain anywhere, though I half expected something in either my head or my chest, a stroke or a heart attack. I was not unduly alarmed since this had become a common occurrence, but this one was more intense than most. I sat down and almost slid off the chair. I held on to the edge of the table in front of me. About then Loretta came in and knew immediately that something was wrong. She said she knew from the panicked expression on my face and the odd angle of my body. We both remembered that Dr. Kinney had told us that sometimes drinking water would help, that becoming slightly dehydrated would adversely affect the balance, so Loretta brought me two or three glasses of water. I sat there for about twenty minutes and the sensation passed. It shook us up.

Well armored with Depends, I went for my talk for that day, at an art museum downtown. I grasped on to the microphone, perched on a low stool, my cane propped over my leg. The audience laughed a lot and applauded wildly when I was finished, though there had been audible gasps when I casually said that Harper Lee was a bitch. I suppose I should not have said that to a bunch of people reading this "beloved" American novel, but I did. Loretta laughed and said I was just trying to be outrageous, but I could tell she didn't approve. Clai and Lydia loved my iconoclasm. Other events followed as the week unfolded; Lydia, Loretta, Mary Ann, and I met with a large group of students and their American lit professor, a young African-American man who had the usual objections to *To Kill a Mockingbird* (all of which I agreed with): its patronizing portrayal of helpless blacks and nice, "good" white folks, the fine, upstanding Atticus Finch's compromising his principles and covering up Boo Radley's crime. I gave a reading from *Coming of Age at the Y*, my first novel, a new paperback edition of which had just been issued. I signed copies of the book. I used up a couple of packages of Depends.

At the end of the week we headed home, Loretta driving the Mercedes, me trying to relax in the passenger seat. We had not tried to make the drive all in one day going down, but we did going home. We were almost to the Alabama state line. I had pissed in my Depends a couple of times, had even remarked to Loretta that this was great, I should have thought of it a long time ago for other trips. I wouldn't have to stop to go to the bathroom all the time. I let loose another warm stream. What I didn't realize was that those goddam things *overflow*! The diaper had filled up, and before I knew what was happening I had wet my clothes, the seat, and the floor carpet of the Benz.

Loretta pulled into an Alabama Welcome Station. We got fresh clothes from the trunk. Thankfully, there was no one there but two black ladies behind the counter, who seemed perplexed when Loretta asked them if they had a family restroom, since she was going to have to come in with me. There was no way I could get undressed, washed up, and then dressed again by myself in a public restroom. They looked at me, leaning on Loretta's shoulder, my pants streaked with tee tee, and I could tell, *again*, they were thinking, "Look at that old drunk white man." I must have smelled to high heaven. But they were sharp. They caught on. They told us to go to a door marked WOMEN, with a yellow sign in front warning that the floor was wet, the restrooms having just been cleaned. They assured us that they would watch and not let anyone in there, as there was another women's room across the hall.

Loretta assisted me in getting undressed. She washed me with paper towels, practically gave me a bath, and we couldn't help but break into gales of giggles. I got dried off and dressed. I tried to walk through the lobby with as much dignity as I could muster. We started laughing again as soon as we got out the door.

All the way to Montevallo we talked sadly about our experience; we decided that this was probably the last time I'd ever be able to do this. I had given readings and done signings for years all over the Southeast, up and down the East Coast, and Loretta and I had loved the travel, Loretta more than me since it was work to me and I didn't enjoy that part of the "writing game" very much. The decade when I was writing plays we practically commuted between Montevallo and New York. Traveling was so much a part of our lives that it had become second nature. But it seemed that we had come to the end of yet another phase in our journey toward growing ever increasingly *old* together.

I would probably never finish those two novels. I was on a cocktail of antidepressants: Wellbutrin and Lexapro in the morning and Trazadone at night. I felt useless, used up. As though it were all over. Loretta's strength and tenderness were palpable.

Twenty-two

One day in Dr. Kinney's office, I felt a tiny ray of hope. Cleve Kinney, a well-respected professor at the medical college at UAB as well as a practitioner, is one of the brightest men I've ever known. In addition to his MD, he has a PhD in neuroanatomy. By this time I had been suffering from the mysterious condition for over three years, and he not only wanted to diagnose my problem, but had been determined all along that something could be done about it. He had been researching and conferring with other doctors, and he explained to me that he thought I didn't have a cyst or a tumor at all, that what I had was a condition called "normal pressure hydrocephalus," an excess of spinal fluid in the brain caused by enlarged ventricles. He showed me on the CT scan. The best thing about NPH is that it can often be corrected by brain surgery.

He recommended that I see Dr. Kristen Riley, a neurosurgeon at Kirklin Clinic at UAB. Dr. Riley inspired immediate confidence in me, and my opinion of her grew as she examined me and looked at my CT scan. Dr. Riley confirmed Dr. Kinney's diagnosis. She explained to Loretta and me that she thought she could reverse all my symptoms with surgery. She would insert a shunt into my brain that would drain the excess fluid through small plastic tubes down to my abdominal cavity, where they would be reabsorbed into my body.

I listened with mounting excitement. She seemed my kind of person: plainspoken and no nonsense. I remarked later that I thought she was a "Hemingway doctor," thinking of the surgeon Rinaldo in *A Farewell to Arms*. She cautioned us that brain surgery was always risky, not to be undertaken lightly, but I didn't care. She said that there was only an 80 percent chance that the surgery would be a success. I liked the odds. I remembered that day in Dr. White's office, thirty years before, when he had told of my 80 percent chance of recovery.

Dr. Riley asked if Loretta and I wanted to think about this at home for a while and then let her know if we wanted to proceed. I told her that no, I didn't need to think about it, I was ready to go.

"Well, when would you like to do it?" she asked.

"As soon as you can," I said. "Right away."

She looked levelly at me. She pulled her appointment book off the desk and scanned through it. She looked up. "I do surgery on Mondays, Wednesdays, and Fridays," she said. "How about tomorrow morning at five thirty? Can you be here?" I looked at Loretta; she smiled and nodded.

"I'll be here," I said.

We were there early the next morning, Loretta letting me out to run into the hospital while she parked the car because I had to piss. I almost made it before I damped my pants, but I could have cared less. Jim Tuohy, our recently retired priest, was there as I was prepped. We were all upbeat, positive. They wheeled me away.

When I gradually awoke in the recovery room, I thought they had put the bandages on my head askew so that they were pulling. It was a while before I realized what I was feeling were the staples in my scalp. I lay there, still floating from the anesthesia. University

Hospital in Birmingham is a vast city hospital, a teaching hospital that covers four city blocks in the downtown area. The recovery room reminded me of scenes in old movies of wounded soldiers in World War I, all lined up in beds. There must have been twenty of us in there. The man in the bed next to mine was naked and covered in the yellow antibiotic they paint on for surgery and he was raging, angry. He wanted to get up and leave. He kept getting out of his bed, and the nurse kept yelling at him, "No, no, you're got a catheter, stay in the bed." I was amused. He obviously had no idea what a catheter was. How in the world could he not know he had one? Or maybe that's why he wanted to get up and leave in a hurry. I lay there thinking that my friend Norman McMillan would get a good laugh hearing about this.

Back in the room, I was relieved and happy. My head was shaved and I had a huge bandage up there. I knew instinctively that I was better. I knew the incontinence had completely gone, but I'm not sure exactly how I could tell. My mind was clear and focused. Dr. Riley came by as the nurse was removing my IV and told me to rest some and then get up and walk after I'd had some lunch. She said I could go home the next day, provided there were no complications. I was giddy. I asked her if she'd called Dr. Kinney and told him the results, and she said she had. I told her to call him back and "tell him to get his ass over here!" She demurred.

I called everybody I could think of. I called Joe and Tricia Taylor in Livingston. I called Clai and Lydia. I called Norman and his wife, Joan. I called my buddy Sid Vance. I even called my friends Sandra and Pat Conroy, but of course I got Pat's machine and his voice mailbox was full. They all said I sounded great and they could tell there had been a drastic change. The staff gave me a normal diet at lunch, and after a nap I got up to walk. I had already gotten up once or twice, with the aid of an orderly, to go to the bathroom, so I knew. I knew! I walked up and down those hospital corridors *without a cane*, only hours after I'd had brain surgery. Loretta fussed at me for walking with the hospital gown open down the back, my ass exposed to the world. "I don't give a fuck!" I said, laughing, too loud. And I didn't. I didn't care if anybody saw me, or if I was too loud. Because I knew that Dr. Kinney and Dr. Riley had saved my life, and I was born again. Again.

The next day was Halloween, 2009, and Norman and Joan McMillan came over and brought us supper. I felt so good that we invited them to stay for drinks and to help us eat it. We invited Meredith to come over and help celebrate. Loretta opened a bottle of good wine. They had removed the bandage from my head before I left the hospital, but it was still slathered in yellow and there was a large gash closed with coppery-looking staples, so I was the one designated to go to the door and give out candy to the trick-or-treaters. I would open the door, hump over, turn my scarred head toward them, wring my hands, cackle ominously, and with a tremulous voice say something like "What can I get for you, my liiiittle goblins?" There were some wide-eyed little witches and monsters who left our door that night.

Dr. Kinney continued me on Aricept and Namenda, though he said my dementia was much diminished and it continued to be very mild. My incontinence did not return. I have not fallen or used a cane since before the surgery. I finished *The Last Queen of the Gypsies* and it was published in 2010 to much praise.

In celebration of my recovery, we took Meredith and the grandchildren on a Mediterranean cruise. Loretta flew to Rome, where she joined her sister, Annette, an artist. They spent three weeks riding the train from Rome, through France to Paris, through the chunnel to Northern England, where they looked up their ancestral home and visited the graves of family members dating back to the twelfth century. Then they took the train through Spain down to Malaga, where they met me, Meredith, Jonathan, and Sara Beth. We boarded the cruise ship and sailed across the beautiful Mediterranean to Rome, where we toured all the sights. We then went up to Florence and Pisa, before sailing over to the incredibly lovely island of Corsica. Then we returned back across the sea and flew home from Malaga.

I have recently signed a contract with Six Finger Publishing, the U.S. branch of a large publishing company with its main offices in the U.K., Great War Literature Publishing, to release eighteen of my short stories digitally, aimed at an academic market. They will come complete with study guides and can be downloaded individually or grouped thematically. The anthology containing all the stories, which I've entitled *Sweet Home: Stories of Alabama*, has also been published. I'm excited about it because the venture allows me to get into the vast, still to me mysterious world of online publishing, while keeping most of my short stories in print. It has also given me the opportunity to go back and reread and polish all those stories and enjoy the rich and varied collection of characters and narratives I've created, that I've contributed to the world. It is very satisfying at this point in my life and my career to be able to see that so clearly.

I have also published a new novel, *A Time to Reap*, about a fractured family during the Vietnam War. Having come from the old school (I wrote my first fledgling stories on an old upright Underwood typewriter, the one I had lugged to Nashville all those years ago), I am astonished at the speed with which publishers in this day and time can bring out a book. The book was launched with a reading and signing at Eclipse Coffee and Books in Montevallo in June 2014.

As I write this, I am hard at work on a "new" novel: a complete rewriting of the Creek Indian book. I am making steady progress. It has turned out to be not so much a novel about the war but a love story encompassing the early days of Demopolis, the story of The Vine and Olive Colony, the subject matter of my early play at Livingston.

My days are up and down, good and bad. On the good days my

mind is clear and sharp and I feel better physically. I am more energetic and my work goes well. On the bad days I am sluggish. I can usually gauge the quality of my day during my morning shower. It takes me much longer to shower and get dressed on the bad days, because I have to *think* about everything. It's not that I don't know what the hairbrush is for, or I've forgotten how to use it; it's just a vacant pause, a hollow moment, almost like my brain has skipped a beat and there has to be a brief, manual correction. Another way of putting it is my "routine" becomes confusing; I get lost in it. On good days, I do the routine with ease, without really thinking about it.

I forget words, simple phrases. People tell me, "Oh, I do that, too! Everybody forgets!" They joke about "old person's disease," what used to be called senility. The difference I notice now: I have always had words slip my mind, but they were usually "just on the tip of my tongue." Everybody has experienced that. Now, however, when I try to recall what something is called, something familiar that I've known all my life—cinnamon, for example, or bow tie—it is not hovering right there, just out of sight. There is a dark empty hole where it used to be. My mind is telling me that I'll never recall it again, and that is frightening.

I have flashes of extremely vivid memories of childhood, a person, a smell, the feel of sunlight on hay, the texture and camphor scent of a quilt—not quilts, but one particular quilt that I slept under at my grandmother's house when I was five years old. I suppose those visions prompted me to write this memoir, to revisit all my old friends and haunts, or as they were referred to at Brookwood Lodge, my old playmates and playgrounds. Reliving all this was gratifying.

But writing it, especially the revision process, was difficult. More and more, as the cloud of dementia begins to creep into the deep recesses of my mind, the things I've always loved to do become harder. The simple process of cutting and pasting was burdensome and challenging. To keep a book-length narrative in my mind at once—something I once did with ease—becomes formidable. It's like a lifetime pianist forgetting how to play. And that is terrifying, because it inevitably will get worse. But I don't let it get me down; I prefer to think of whatever is going to happen as my next big adventure in life.

I watched my father's dementia take over his life, his consciousness, so that he existed on some plane divorced from the world around him. The creativeness of his demented visions haunts me. It was as if he were inventing and actualizing a parallel history, his own distorted narrative, another existence in which men were forever failing to pay him the money they owed him for the farm equipment he continued to sell. Other men were shooting at him with some elaborate ray gun from up in Tennessee, attempting to kill him; he told me with deliberate seriousness, a Lear-like madness in his eyes—my own dark brown eyes—that they had already killed his brother, my Uncle Oscar, who had died of cancer some fifteen years before, and would be after me next. I knew where the Tennessee obsession came from. He had once told me that when he was a little boy, he had slept in the same room with his Grandpa Nunnery. One of the old man's legs had been shot off in the Battle of Franklin, in Tennessee, and my father used to help him rub lineament on his stump. Mr. Nunnery's job around the place was caring for the garden; one day he came onto the back porch where my father was, put a bowl of plump ripe strawberries on the table, and fell over dead.

There was an astonishing logic to his hallucinations. The dark mystery of cancer, beyond his understanding and against which he was helpless, had taken his mother, his daughter, his brother. Perhaps the novel his mind was writing for him was his last attempt at supplying answers to the questions that had plagued him all his life, to give form to the chaos of his life. Which is what all fiction, all myth, all stories attempt to do—from Homer to the New Testament, from the great novels and epics of our culture down to the meager scribblings of a writer like me. My father, in his own feverish dreams at the end, wrote his own story: a fictional one to be sure, one that was not "real," but like all great fiction, one truer than the mere facts of his life.

I'm certain the old Red and Black Bullet long ago went to that great junkyard in the sky, but in my mind and my memories it is still moving along, going too fast down that county road, with Captain Billy's Troopers packed inside, singing at the tops of their voices. They are all in there: Lester and Donald, Loretta, Clem and Eleanor, Bobby, Sally, Richard, Angie, Byrd, all crammed in, even those who—Pat, Jayne, Winston, William—are now gone from this earth.

There are at least a thousand other people I could have taken along for this journey, all in one way or the other Troopers, too, fellow riders of the night. They have all touched my life in great ways and small. But this is not the story of that entire, long life; I'm afraid much too much of it would be taken up by day after day after day of "hair of the dog," secret sips, frantic lies, desperate attempts at quitting drinking that only failed. And then, after my sobriety, there was the drudgery of "one day at a time," my not very dramatic or interesting struggle over time not to drink.

No. This is only the story of that life's heart and core. One man's stagger toward recovery.

I remember one day several years before William Meredith died, in one of those long bull sessions he and I would have, when the talk had turned to literary reputation and William looked at me and smiled. "You and me," he said, "you and me," pointing first at me and then at his chest. He chuckled. "After we're dead," he said in his halting way, smiling through the stroke-induced strictures of his face. I knew what he meant. We laughed together. It was a pact with which we were both comfortable.